Nan Mensinga-Biasiny

BEAUTIFUL BABY CLOTHES

To Crochet, Knit, Sew and Embroider

Photography by
Charles Biasiny-Rivera

Drawings by the author

Simon and Schuster • New York

Published by Simon and Schuster
A Division of Gulf & Western Corporation
Simon & Schuster Building
Rockefeller Center
1230 Avenue of the Americas
New York, New York 10020

All photographs by Charles Biasiny-Rivera except those of the four buntings mentioned above, which are by Frances McLaughlin-Gill.

Designed by Eve Metz
Manufactured in the United States of America

1 2 3 4 5 6 7 8 9 10

Library of Congress Cataloging in Publication Data

Mensinga-Biasiny, Nan.
Beautiful baby clothes to crochet, knit, sew, and embroider.

1. Infants—Clothing. 2. Sewing. 3. Fancy work. I. Title.
TT637.M46 746.9'2 76-51753

ISBN 0-671-22467-0

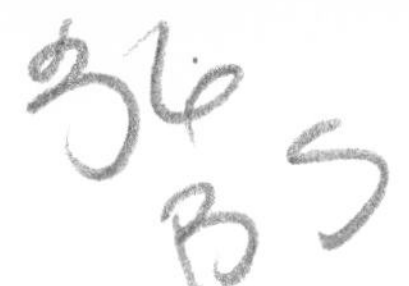

TO NIKOLA

A heartfelt thank you to those who enthusiastically helped me in the making of this book: first and foremost my husband, Charles, for taking the beautiful photographs; Jacqueline Olsen, whose nimble fingers knitted many of the garments; Gwen Benson, for the expert sewing job she did, Rosemary Drysdale for embroidering the peasant blanket and bunting, and Nan Rullo for her help.

Then, of course, there are the babies, who contributed so much by just being their lovely, smiling selves: Holly Edelson, Chi Richardson, Cara Schnitzer, Alejandro Tracy-Raeder, Marcos Daniel Smith, Shannon Plaine, Melissa Mabuchi and their mothers.

Last, but certainly not least, Julie Houston, for being such a patient editor.

Contents

Contents

NOTE TO THE MOTHER-TO-BE

Suddenly, now that you are pregnant, you want to start making things for the little being that's growing day by day inside you. Even if you have never touched a hook or needle in your life, this is the challenge you have been waiting for.

If this is your first pregnancy, nine months may seem like an almost endless time. Enjoy it, daydream and plan ahead.

It is such a nice feeling to make your own baby clothes. Needless to say it will save you money, since buying them can add up considerably. But above all, it is fun and you'll feel terribly creative.

Here is a collection of all those special things you'll want to make. Almost the entire collection of clothes to make for babies, from birth to one year, has been based on very basic shapes—squares, rectangles, circles, **L** and **T** shapes—which I hope will also help you to do your own thing. In many cases, suggestions have been given for variations of the same designs.

Even if you are a beginner or a slowpoke, many small items will be easy and quick to make. Sew some receiving blankets, or kimonos of soft flannel, or decorate an undershirt to your heart's content. Then with your confidence bolstered, you'll want to tackle something more ambitious. From a couple of skeins of yarn or a yard of pretty fabric, you can make a warm blanket, soft little booties, kimonos delicately trimmed with crochet, a cozy bunting for snowy days or a cool little embroidered peasant smock.

For baby clothes, practicality should be kept in mind as a major factor. No one wants to get bogged down in ironing and handwashing when it is so much more important to spend that time with your baby. Today with all the available perma-press fabrics and synthetic yarns, you should be able to make a completely machine-washable wardrobe. But don't let practicality keep you from making that special outfit or heirloom christening dress which requires tender loving care.

Of course, you're not the only one who will want to make things. As soon as the word "baby" is out, friends and relatives will get into action and pick up their hooks and needles. Parties will be planned, showers given, and what could be more welcome than an "I made it myself" gift?

Even though science has taken us to the moon and back, we still have no way to know whether you will have a boy or girl. So, although pink and blue are still the traditional baby colors, be daring in your color scheme. Try something different—mint, lavender, yellow or whatever color appeals to you. Just imagine black or red velvet against that exquisite baby skin.

When the last month rolls around, your bassinet will be all made up and waiting and you will be counting the days while busy putting all those little kimonos, dresses and gowns—so lovingly made—into the freshly lined dresser drawers. As you tuck a fragrant sachet here and there, you will feel really ready for the great event.

Your life will never be the same. Above all enjoy, enjoy this exciting time. The first year goes by so quickly.

General How-To

The wonderful thing about needlecraft is that you don't have to spend a fortune to equip yourself for many an enjoyable hour making these baby clothes.

EQUIPMENT

CROCHET HOOKS: Crochet hooks come in many sizes and are made of a variety of materials.

Steel crochet hooks are used for the finer cotton threads and range in size from 00, the largest, to 14, a hair-fine hook.

Aluminum or plastic hooks are used for both wool and cotton, and are often recommended for the beginner. They are usually sized from B through K, or numbered from 1 through 10½—K and 10½ being the largest.

Afghan hooks are specially made to execute the afghan stitch. They are about 9″ to 14″ long and are meant to hold a large number of stitches. They are sized in the same manner as other crochet hooks.

Since hooks are sized differently by the various manufacturers—some by letter, some by number—it is wise to select from well- and widely distributed brand names.

The sizing of hooks is not the same in the United States, as in Canada and England. Here is a listing of comparative sizes:

STEEL HOOKS

American	English/Canadian
00	
0	
1	0
2	1
3	1½
4	2
5	2½
6	3
7	3½
8	4
9	4½
10	5
11	5½
12	6
13	6½
14	7

ALUMINUM OR PLASTIC HOOKS

American	English/Canadian
B-1	14
C-2	13
D-3	12
E-4	11
F-5	10
G-6	9
H-7	8
I-8	7
J-9	6
K-10½	4

KNITTING NEEDLES: These are also made of different materials, such as steel, aluminum, plastic and wood, and come in a variety of sizes and lengths.

Straight needles with single points are used for working back and forth in rows. They are sold in pairs, in 10″ and 14″ lengths.

Double pointed needles come in sets of 4, in 7″ and 9″ lengths. They are used for socks, mittens, hats and other items worked in the round.

Circular needles are used for knitting seamless garments such as skirts, socks or mittens. However, you can also knit back and forth on a circular needle as you would with straight needles, a useful method when the piece has too many stitches to fit on a straight needle. Circular needles come in the regular sizes and in 11″ to 36″ lengths.

The sizes of hooks and needles are specified in the directions of each project in this book, but in general needles and hooks are chosen to suit the type of work you are doing and the yarn you are using. The length of the needle is mainly determined by the number of stitches it will have to hold.

Needle sizes are indicated by numbers. The standardization of knitting needles leaves as much to be desired as for crochet hooks. So, the same guideline applies here: buy well-distributed, well-known brand names.

A listing of comparative sizes for the United States, England and Canada is given below, size 15 and 000 being the largest.

American:
0 - 1 - 2 - 3 - 4 - 5 - 6 - 7 - 8 - 9 - 10 - 11 - 13 - 15
English/Canadian:
13 - 12 - 11 - 10 - 9 - 8 - 7 - 6 - 5 - 4 - 3 - 2 - 0 - 000

RING MARKERS are small plastic or metal rings used to separate sections of work where patterns are to be worked, or to indicate where increases or decreases are to be made.

RULER OR TAPE MEASURE is necessary to check your gauge, or to find out how far you have to work.

TAPESTRY NEEDLE is a large-eyed, blunt-pointed needle used for sewing seams, weaving 2 sections together and working embroidery over an afghan-stitch background. The blunt point will prevent you from splitting the yarn.

MATERIALS

Today there are many different kinds of yarn to choose from in a rainbow of colors, with new and unusual textures, made of natural or synthetic fibers.

For baby clothes the washability of the yarn you select will be a major factor in deciding what kind of yarn to buy.

When you buy yarn, always buy enough to complete the entire garment and check that the dye-lot numbers are the same on all the labels. (A dye lot number refers to a quantity of yarn dyed at the same time in the same dye bath.) There is always a color variation, however slight, between two dye lots, which will always be visible in your work and may spoil its looks.

The yarns and threads mentioned in the directions have been specially chosen to suit the design. Unless you are an experienced needleworker, do *not* substitute them for other yarns since they have been knitted or crocheted to a specific gauge on a specific size needle or hook, to obtain the desired and correct size.

Now that we are slowly changing over to a metric system, here is a conversion chart:

Weights:	28 grams	= about 1 oz.
	50 grams	= about 1¾ oz.
	100 grams	= about 3½ oz.
Measurements:	6 mm	= ¼″
	1.3 cm	= ½″
	2.5 cm	= 1″
	90 cm	= 35–36″
	115 cm	= 44–45″

GAUGE

At the beginning of all knitting and crochet directions, a gauge is given. This simply means the number of stitches and number of rows per inch.

I cannot stress enough how important it is that you work exactly to the gauge indicated in the directions, so that your garment will be the correct size.

Before you start the actual item, check *your* gauge by making a practice swatch about 4″ square, using the yarn and hook or needle size specified in the directions. If you get the same number of stitches and rows as indicated in the directions, you are working to the *same* gauge, and you can go ahead and work the design on the size hook or needle indicated.

However, if the number of stitches and rows per inch do not correspond, you have to try a different size hook or needle. The way you work is very personal and you cannot really make an effort to change your tension and still work comfortably.

The size of hook or needle you use is not important as long as you obtain the correct gauge.

If you have *more* stitches to the inch than specified, you work tighter and you should try a *larger* hook or needle.

If you have *fewer* stitches, you are working more loosely and should try using a *smaller* hook or needle.

Keep changing the size hook or needle, until you obtain the exact gauge as specified.

TO MAKE THE CORRECT SIZE

Nothing is less exact than the sizing for babies under one year old. Their weights at birth vary and what fits one baby at six months may not fit another one at all. So, as many measurements as possible have been indicated on each garment against which to check your baby's measurements. Just remember, a little too big never hurts. The baby will always grow into it.

HOW TO READ INSTRUCTIONS

It is always a good idea to read the directions from beginning to end before you start. If you come across a technique you are not familiar with, try it out first. Make a swatch big enough to repeat the pattern a couple of times; for example, if a pattern is a "multiple of 6 plus 3," work your swatch over $(2 \times 6 + 3 =)$ 15 stitches. Especially watch out for phrases such as "and at the same time . . ."

Always mark where you've left off in your directions when you put your work down. It is also helpful to place a ruler or a strip of cardboard on the directions below the row you are working on. That way, you can't skip a row, or jump to the wrong one when you are glancing from your work to the directions.

HOW TO READ CHARTS

When working cross-stitch patterns, Fair Isle knitting or when crocheting a design, a chart is given with the directions. Follow the charts for the design and the key for colors, considering each little square on the chart as one stitch in your work. When knitting or crocheting, follow the chart from right to left on right side of work and from left to right on wrong side of work.

ABBREVIATIONS

These seem to present the biggest stumbling block for the beginner. Trying to follow directions is really not as complicated as it looks. Abbreviations are necessary for space's sake. Otherwise, instruction books would be twice their size.

Here are the most commonly used abbreviations and an explanation of the terms and symbols most often used in crochet and knitting.

Crochet Abbreviations

Beg—beginning of a row or round
Bl—block
Ch—chain
Cl—cluster
Dc—double crochet
Dec—decrease
Dpl—double picot loop
Dtr—double treble
Hdc—half double crochet
Hk—hook
Inc—increase
Incl—inclusive
Lp(s)—loop(s)
P—picot
Patt—pattern
Rep—repeat
Rnd—round
Sc—single crochet
Sk—skip
Sl—slip
Sl st—slip stitch
Sp(s)—space(s)
St(s)—stitch(es)
Tog—together
Tr—treble

Tr tr—triple treble
Y o—yarn (thread) over hook

Knitting Abbreviations
Beg—beginning of a row or round
Dec—decrease
Dp—double pointed (needles)
Inc—increase
K—knit
K-wise—knit-wise, as if to knit
P—purl
Patt—pattern
Psso—pull or pass the slipped stitch over the next stitch
P-wise—purl-wise, as if to purl
Rep—repeat
Rnd—round
Sk—skip
Sl—slip a stitch from left-hand needle to right-hand needle as if to purl without working it
Sl st—slip stitch
St(s)—stitch(es)
Sl 1, k 1, psso—slip 1 stitch, knit 1 stitch and pull the slipped stitch over the knit stitch
Sl 1, y f (b)—slip 1 stitch holding yarn in front (back) of work
Sl 1, k 2 tog, psso—slip 1 stitch, knit 2 stitches together and pass the slipped stitch over the 1 stitch resulting from the 2 stitches knitted together
Tog—together
Y o—yarn (or thread) over; wrap yarn over the needle to make a new stitch

TERMS AND SYMBOLS

* - **Asterisk**—This means repeat the instructions following the asterisk as many times as specified *in addition to* the first time.
( ) - **Parentheses**—This means repeat instructions in parentheses as many times as specified. For instance (ch 7, dc in next dc) 5 times, or (k 1, p 1) 5 times, means to work all that is in parentheses 5 times *in all.*
Even—When directions say "work even," that means to continue working in pattern as established without increasing or decreasing.
Multiple of stitches—A pattern often needs an exact number

of stitches to complete. This means that the number of stitches you are working on must be divisible by this number; for example, multiple of 4 would be 8, 12, 16, 20, etc. Multiple of 4 plus 3 would be 11, 15, 19, 23, etc.

Place a marker in work—This means to mark a certain point in the work itself with a pin or thread, to use as a guide in measuring your work, or as a point to refer back to later. Or, if you are working in rounds, to mark the beginning of each round.

Place a marker on needle (for knitting only)—You actually place a marker in the form of a little ring on the needle itself, between stitches. The marker is slipped from one needle to the other as you work across the row.

YARN BOBBINS

When you are knitting or crocheting an item in more than one color, and a design is to be worked, which is not repeated continuously across the row (as, for example, in Fair Isle knitting, where the colors change every few stitches), a bobbin of yarn is attached where indicated, to work each color of the motif.

You can make your own bobbins, feather-light little woolen balls, that pull from the center, an ingenious Scottish method, instead of winding yarn around plastic bobbins, which easily get entangled.

This is how you make them:

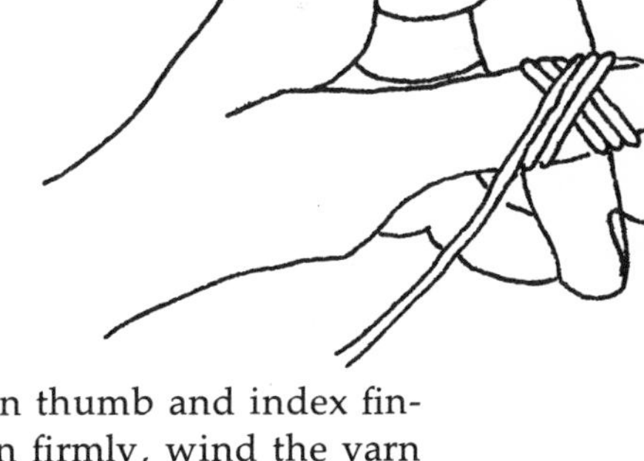

Hold yarn in your left hand, between thumb and index finger. While holding the free end of yarn firmly, wind the yarn with your right hand around the left thumb at different angles until you have a small amount. Remove ball of yarn from thumb and continue winding at different angles, being careful not to catch the free end into the windings. Break off and slip end under last winding. The free end will pull from the center of the bobbin.

When the yarn has been almost used up, the bobbin falls apart and you have to rewind it. Rewind the ball as before, starting with the end that is attached to your work.

TO ENLARGE PATTERNS AND DIAGRAMS TO ACTUAL SIZE

You will need a pencil, ruler, tissue paper and sheets of brown paper as large as the length and width of the item you are going to make. (**Note:** Cut open a brown paper shopping bag and iron it flat with a hot iron.)

Make a grid as follows: With dots, mark off the necessary inches for the square or rectangle needed, making sure the corners are true (that is, at an exact 90-degree angle). Then mark dots 1″ apart around 4 sides. With a ruler, draw horizontal and vertical lines between the dots across opposite sides of the paper. Make sure you have the same number of squares on the grid as there are squares on the pattern diagram.

Now copy the design or pattern from the original, line for line, square by square, on the grid, and your pattern or design will be enlarged to full size.

If you don't want to go through the trouble of making your own grid, buy sheets of 1″ graph paper at an art-supply store.

CUTTING AND SEWING PATTERNS

Enlarge the patterns to actual size following the instructions above. Make a tissue paper tracing of each pattern piece on the grid. Mark all pattern pieces "front, back, sleeve, pocket . . ." etc., and indicate such instructions as "fold, cut 2 . . ." etc.

The outline of the pattern piece is the actual *cutting* line of the pattern; ½″ seam and hem allowances are included, unless otherwise specified.

Baste seams before stitching them.

Clip curves where necessary.

Press all seams open and flat.

Finish raw edges with overhand stitch to prevent unraveling.

FINISHING

WASHING A HANDKNITTED OR CROCHETED GARMENT: Considering the fact that most of the items in this book are small and many hours of tender loving care will have gone into their making, you should try to handwash them. It is always the safest rule for washing 100 percent wool, cotton or synthetic yarns alike. Use lukewarm water and a good quality soap which dissolves well in low-temperature water.

Or, make thick suds with soap flakes and hot water, then add cold water until it is lukewarm.

Squeeze the suds through the garment several times. Do not rub or twist. Wash and rinse until all the soap has been rinsed out.

Squeeze water out; NEVER wring. To remove any excess water, roll tightly in a thick bath towel and push down on it. Spread garment flat on a dry towel (never hang up a wet garment; the weight of the water will pull it out of shape), and with a tuck here and there shape the article according to the measurements indicated.

Synthetic yarns do not have the "crimp" (that is, the natural elasticity) of 100 percent wool and therefore need more careful shaping after washing.

Never dry the garment near artificial heat or in direct sunlight. Discoloration and shrinkage may occur.

There are many new types of yarn on the market—natural, synthetic, a combination of fibers, specially treated 100 percent wool yarns, all machine washable and dryable—and manufacturers print laundering instructions on the label, so it is important to read them carefully.

Note: You do not have to wash your work before blocking and sewing if you have kept it clean. One way of keeping it clean is to wash your hands each time before picking up your work—especially when you are working with light-colored yarns—and keeping your work in a plastic bag or pillowcase to keep the dust and dirt out.

BLOCKING

This means steaming, pressing and shaping the parts of an article to the size and measurements given in the directions, *before* sewing it together. If you have washed your work, block while it is still damp.

If a garment consists of several pieces, block similar pieces together. That way they will be exactly the same size; for example, two fronts or two sleeves should be blocked together.

You lay the pieces to be blocked with wrong side up (or two similar pieces with right sides of work together) on a padded surface. Using RUSTPROOF pins, pin the pieces out to the measurements given, placing the pins ¼″ apart all around the outer edges.

If your work is still damp, place a dry, clean cloth over it. If the work is dry, use a damp cloth. On a smooth surface such as stockinette stitch and single crochet, press the hot iron very gently on the cloth, being careful not to let the weight of the iron rest on the work. Do it quickly so as not to dry out the pressing cloth. Let your work dry thoroughly before unpinning it.

Of course, if items are worked in any raised pattern or fluffy yarn, they should be steamed and not pressed. Pin out the work as before, hold a steam iron as close as possible above the work. Without touching the work, move the steam iron around above it. Again, unpin when it is completely dry. Or you may not have to use an iron at all. Pin out the work as described and, with a plant mister or spray bottle, dampen your work well, let dry and unpin, and that's all.

SEWING SEAMS

Seams should be sewn as invisible as possible with minimum bulkiness, especially on small baby items. On a knitted item it is often possible to weave stitches together in an invisible manner (see kitchener stitch, page 81). When pinning pieces together to be sewn, be careful to match stripes, pattern or stitch rows.

Always use the yarn the item is made of to assemble the garment, using a tapestry needle for sewing.

Sometimes, when a garment is made of knitting worsted, you can get a less bulky seam by splitting the yarn. Knitting yarn consists of 4 threads of yarn (4-ply) that are twisted together. Untwist the length of yarn needed and use only 2 strands to sew with.

Backstitching is the most common method of sewing seams in handknits. Pin the pieces to be sewn with right sides together and backstitch close to edge, being careful not to pull the yarn too tight; otherwise work will pucker.

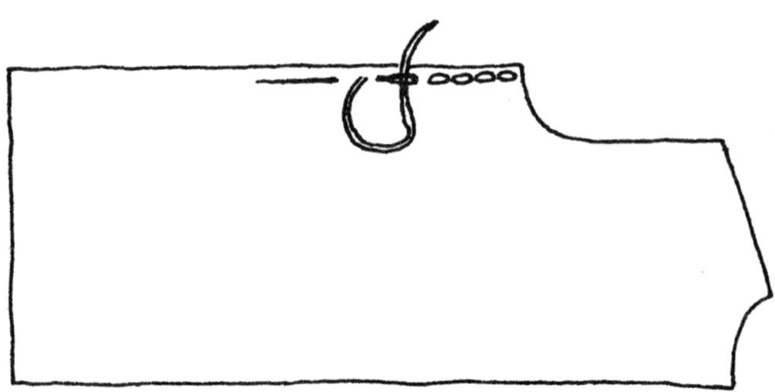

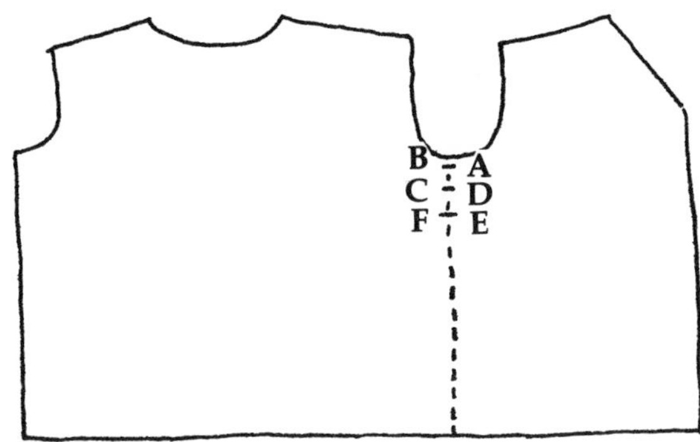

Overhand stitch Place 2 edges to be sewn side by side, with right side of work facing you, flat on a surface. Bring needle and thread from wrong side up through the top stitch of front (A on diagram) to the right side, insert needle from right side through topstitch of back (B on diagram) and bring it out to right side of work about 1/8" below B at C on diagram. Insert needle from right side of work 1/8" below A (at D on diagram) on front and bring it out 1/8" below point where you inserted needle last (E on diagram). Insert needle from right side of work 1/8" below C at F on diagram, and bring it up again 1/8" below point where you inserted needle last. Continue in this manner until seam is completed. This gives you a nice smooth and flat seam.

POMPOMS

Cut 2 cardboard circles 1½ times the desired size of the pompom (for example, for a 2" pompom cut a circle 3" in diameter). Cut a hole in center of both circles, always 1/3 of the total diameter. Place circles together. Wind strands of yarn through center opening and around cardboard circles until center hole is filled.

Slip scissor point between circles and cut all strands at outside edge. Carefully slide a strand of yarn between circles and wind a couple of times very tightly around center of clipped strands; knot, leaving a long enough end to attach pompom. Remove cardboard circles. Fluff up pompom and trim uneven areas.

TASSELS

Cut a cardboard rectangle the desired length of tassel and wind yarn around it as many times to obtain the fullness you want. Slip a length of yarn under strands at one end of cardboard and knot tightly. Slide yarn from cardboard and cut loops at opposite end. Wrap a length of yarn a couple of times around top of tassel below tie. Knot.

TWISTED CORD

Cut a number of strands of yarn. The number of strands should be half the number of strands needed for the required thickness of the completed cord (for example, if you want a 4-strand cord, cut 2 strands 2½ times the desired length). Twist these strands tightly until they kink. Double the twisted cord, and let it twist around itself. Knot ends and trim.

Crocheted Clothes

With a little hook and some yarn, you are ready to embark on one of the simplest, yet most creative of needlecrafts. Basically, all you do with that little hook is to pull one loop of yarn through another loop. It does not always require great concentration and, since baby clothes are small, take your work along wherever you go, making use of those otherwise lost moments on bus or waiting in the doctor's office.

Whether you are a novice or experienced crocheter, you'll find something to your liking here to make. There is an easy-to-make two-piece outfit, a T-shirt with matching pants and a flannel kimono delicately trimmed in crochet with matching booties for a new baby. Spruce up the bassinet with gingham sheets and a pillowcase edged in filet crochet for a charming country look. To keep the baby warm and cozy, there is a bunting in a handsome geometric design, a blanket embroidered with brightly colored flowers, a fashionable afghan coat for a sophisticated one-year-old and much more—to make for your baby or to give as a present.

TECHNIQUES

Yarn and hook size are specified for each project. Before you start, it is important that you check your gauge according to the directions on page 17.

If you have any trouble following directions, see pp. 18–21 for an explanation of terms and what the abbreviations stand for.

When you have completed your project, check pp. 22–25 on how to finish it; that is, washing, blocking and assembling.

TO INCREASE: Work 2 stitches in 1 stitch. This gives you 1 extra stitch.

TO DECREASE A SINGLE CROCHET: Work a single crochet to the point where there are 2 loops on the hook. Draw up a loop in the next stitch, yarn over hook, and draw yarn through all 3 loops on hook.

TO DECREASE A DOUBLE CROCHET: Work a double crochet to the point where there are 2 loops on the hook. Begin another double crochet in the next stitch, and work until there are 4 loops on the hook. Yarn over hook and draw through 2 loops. Yarn over hook again and draw through 3 remaining loops on the hook.

TURNING YOUR WORK: Different stitches vary in length, and each one needs a different number of chain stitches at the end of a row in order to turn and obtain the same length on the next row.

Here is a table which gives you the number of chain stitches needed to turn for each stitch:

Single crochet	—ch 1, turn
Half double crochet	—ch 2, turn
Double crochet	—ch 3, turn
Treble crochet	—ch 4, turn

TO OBTAIN THE CORRECT NUMBER OF STITCHES: When you are designing your own project, here is a little rule of thumb to help you calculate how many chain stitches you need on a foundation chain in order to obtain a particular number of stitches.

If you need 9 single crochet stitches: chain 10, and single crochet in the second chain from hook and in each chain across.

If you need 8 double crochet stitches: chain 10, and double crochet in the fourth chain from hook and in each chain across. Count the turning chain as 1 double crochet. The turning chain consists of the first 3 stitches skipped at the beginning.

THE AFGHAN STITCH: Using an afghan hook, this stitch is always worked first from right to left, picking up loops on the foundation chain and on the return row from left to right, working off the loops. This counts as 1 row.

If you are not familiar with this stitch, chain 20 to make a sample swatch. Work as follows:

Insert hook under 2 top threads of second chain from hook, yarn over and draw a loop through that chain.

Keeping all the loops you pull up on the hook, draw up a loop in each remaining chain stitch. There should now be 20 loops on your hook. Now that all the loops are on the hook, yarn over and draw through the first loop, yarn over, and draw through the next 2 loops, * yarn over, draw through the following 2 loops. Repeat from * across the row. The first row has been completed and 20 vertical bars are made. The loop that remains on the hook at the end of the row is always counted as the first stitch of the next row. Do not turn your work.

To begin the next and succeeding rows, insert your hook under the second vertical bar and pull up a loop. Continue to draw up loops under each vertical bar across to within the last vertical bar. Insert the hook through double loop of last stitch and draw up a loop. By working the last stitch in this manner, you will keep a firm edge.

Work off all the loops as before, drawing through 1 loop first and then through 2 loops at a time across the row.

On the last row, working from right to left, make a slip stitch in each vertical bar to keep the top edge of work flat.

To Increase an Afghan Stitch: Pull up a loop in the horizontal chain between 2 vertical bars.

To Decrease an Afghan Stitch: Insert your hook under 2 vertical bars and pull up 1 loop.

CROSS-STITCH EMBROIDERY OVER AFGHAN STITCH BACKGROUND: Because the afghan stitch forms an almost perfect square, it is an ideal background to work cross-stitch embroidery on. See diagram below. Check page 74 on how to execute the cross-stitch itself.

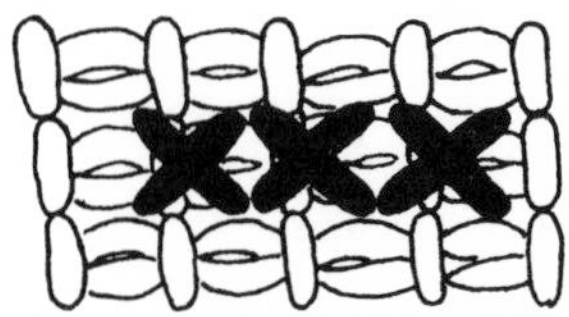

CROCHETING WITH MORE THAN ONE COLOR: There are 2 methods of doing this:

To Change Colors at the End of a Row: Break off the old color, leaving a long enough end to weave in. Tie on the new color with a slipknot and move knot close to the edge of your work. Make a turning chain with the new color and turn work.

Or, work to within last stitch in the old color. With old color, work the last stitch, whether it is a single or double crochet, to the point where there are 2 loops on the hook. Pick up the new color, yarn over with new color and complete stitch. Break off the old color, leaving a long enough end to weave in. With the new color, make the appropriate turning chain and turn work.

To Change Colors Within a Pattern Row: Work to within the last stitch in the first color group. With first color, work until there are 2 loops on the hook. Drop the first color, pick up new color. Yarn over with new color and complete the last stitch in the first color group. Continue with new color, holding color not in use along top edge of previous row, on the wrong side of the work, and crochet over it in such a manner that the unused color is hidden within the stitches of the new color.

If you work a motif that is not repeated across the row, attach a bobbin to complete it. To make yarn bobbins, see page 21.

REVERSE SINGLE CROCHET: This method is often used to give a nice, rounded finishing touch to an edge.

Attach the yarn to work with a slip stitch. Working from *left to right,* insert the hook in the edge of work to the right of the slip stitch, pull up a loop (2 loops on hook), * yarn over, draw yarn through 2 loops on hook, insert hook in work to right of last single crochet made and repeat from * across edge.

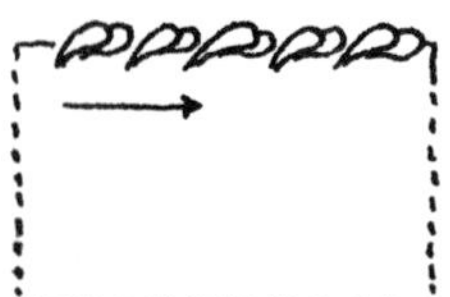

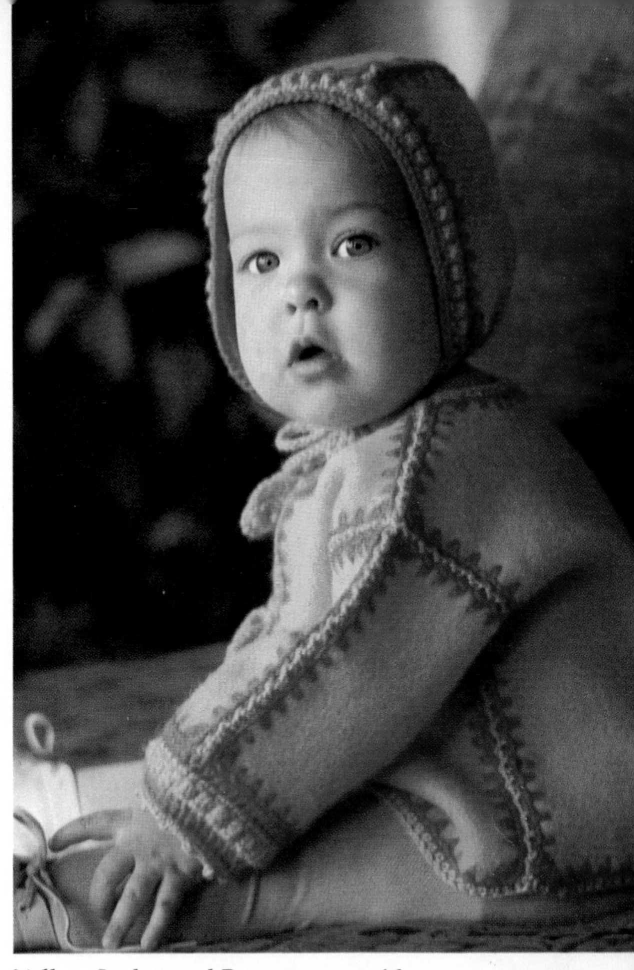

Yellow Jacket and Bonnet, page 46

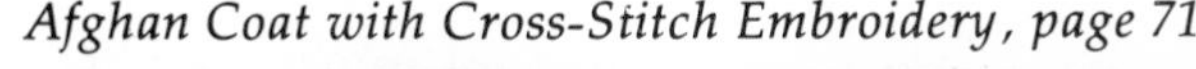

Afghan Coat with Cross-Stitch Embroidery, page 71

Striped Tank Top and Soakers, page 83

T-Shirt and Soakers, page 43

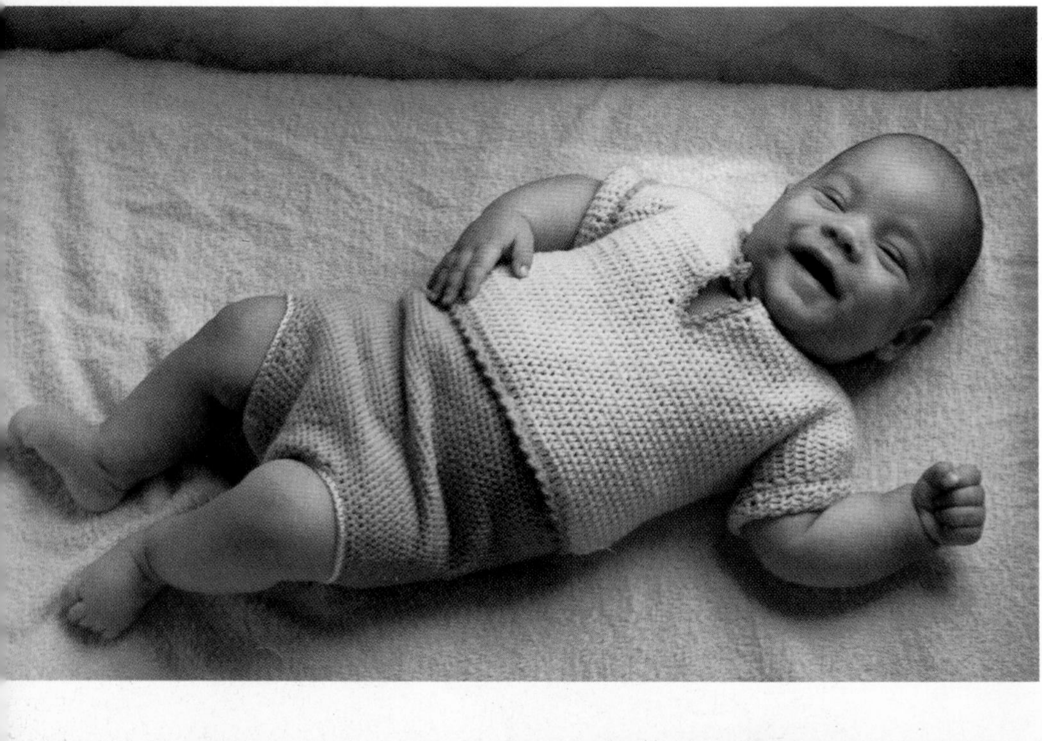

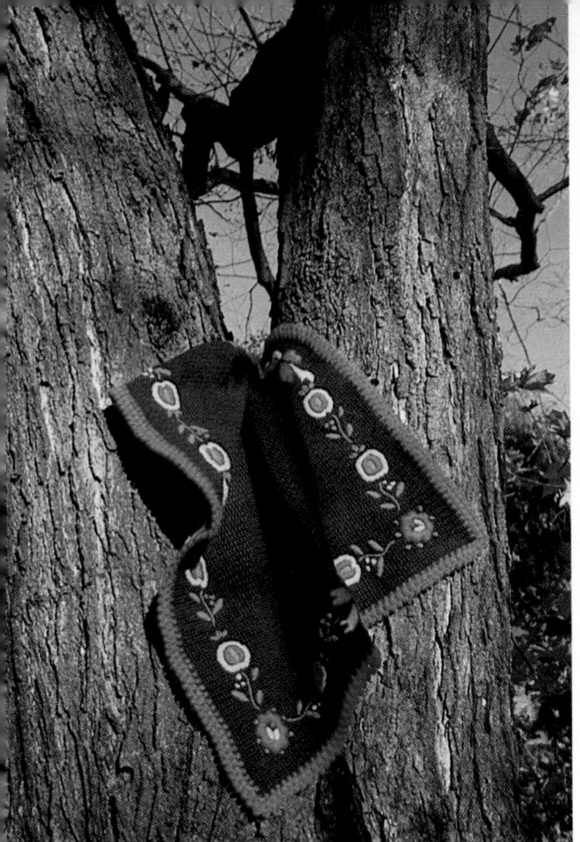

Peasant Blanket, page 41

Bassinet Set, page 53

(Left) *Bunting in Geometric Design, page 66;* (right) *Embroidered Bunting, page 152*

Dress in Variegated Yarn, page 95

Three-Piece Quilted Calico Set, page 127

(Left) *Royal Blue Bunting, page 109;* (right) *Tweed Bunting, page 145*

Red Heart Pincushion, page 147

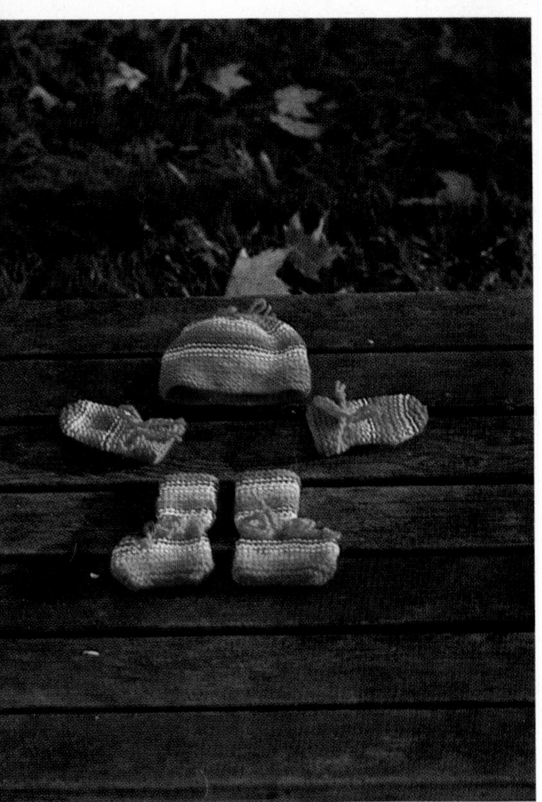

Hat, Mittens and Booties Set, page 86

Norwegian Sleeper, page 106

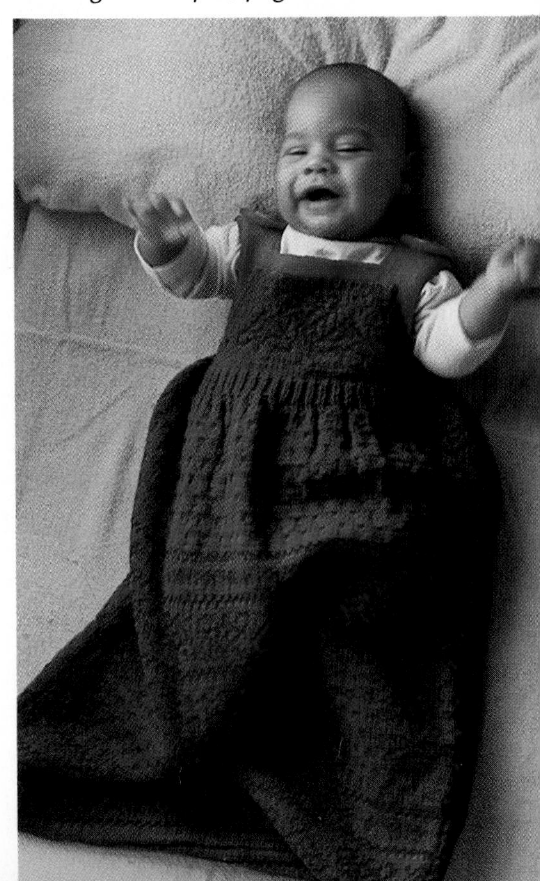

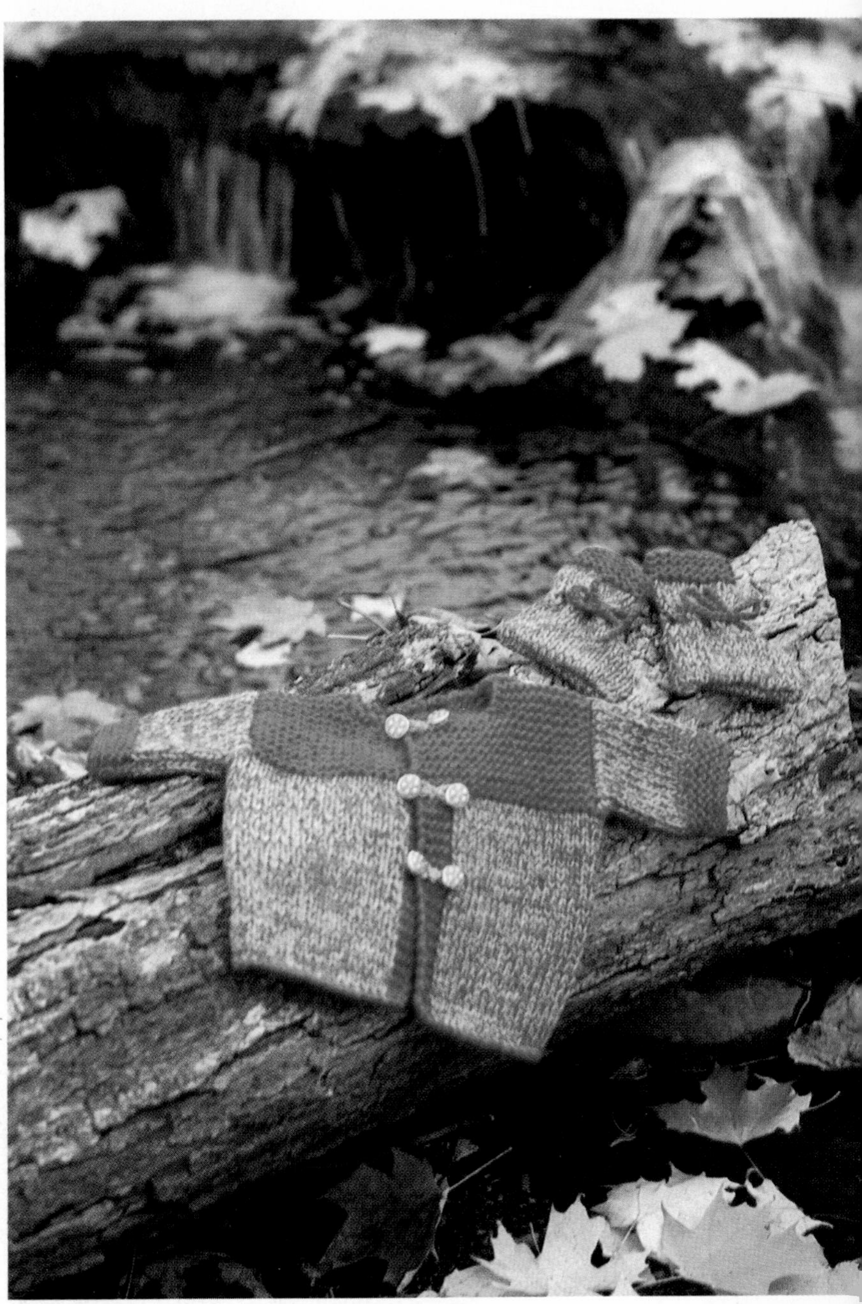

A Warm Woolen Jacket and Booties, page 88

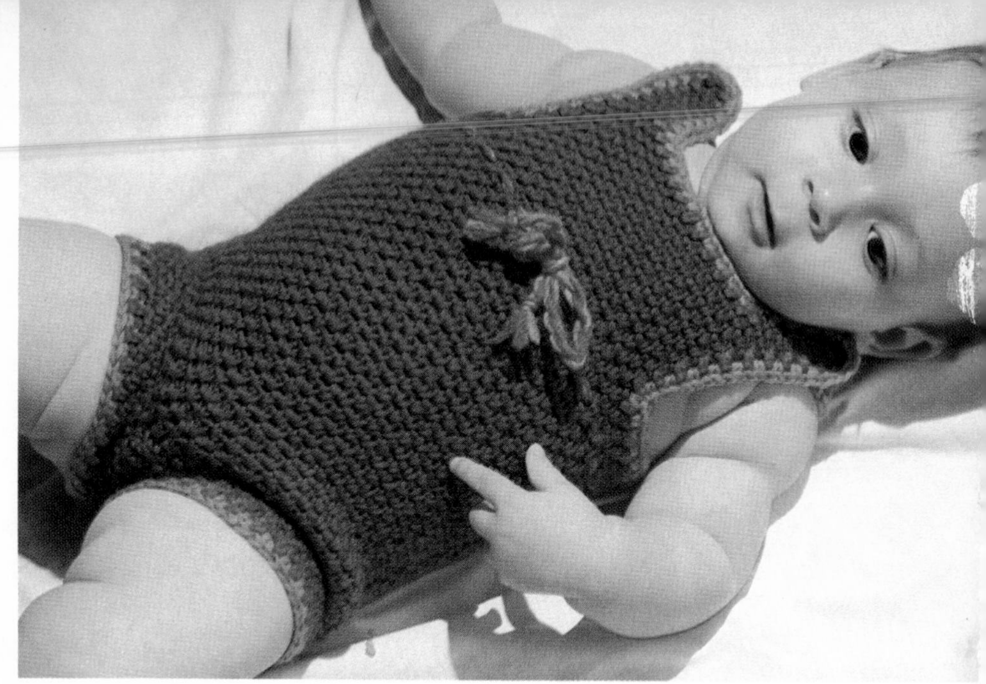

Sunsuit, page 39

Swiss Smock, page 142

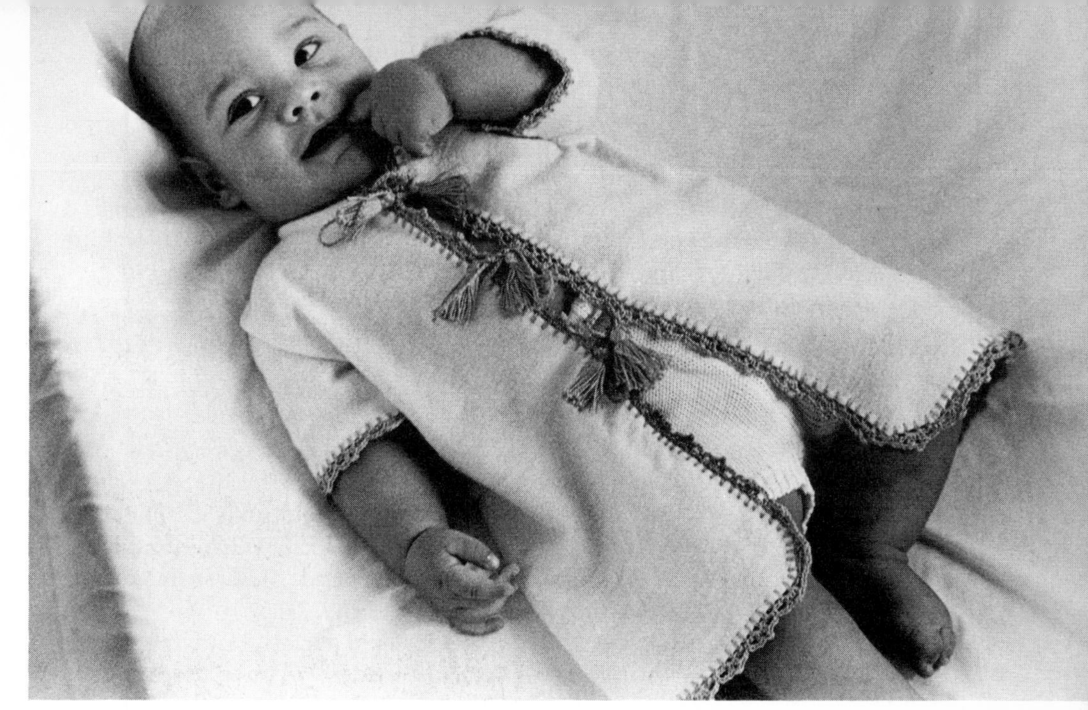

BABY BLUE KIMONO AND SLIPPERS

Here is an easy-to-make blue cotton flannel kimono, trimmed with a blue pearl cotton crocheted edging, with slippers to match. The set is worked in single and double crochet with a flowered toe motif.

The kimono would be nice and cool for summer when made of 100 percent cotton fabric.

If you want to make this as a gift set, add a receiving blanket to match. This is a 36-inch square of flannel or cotton. Hem the edges, and crochet edging to match, in the same manner as for the kimono. Just remember, you will need a multiple of 4 loops (for an explanation of "multiple" see page 20) to work the scallop pattern evenly around.

SIZE: Infant. Kimono measures 12″ across back at underarms, 17″ from back neck to lower edge. Side seam is 11½″, sleeve length, 3″. Slippers measure 3½″ from heel to toe.

MATERIALS: ¾ yd. of 45″-wide baby blue cotton flannel; 4 (50-yd.) balls Coats and Clark's Pearl cotton no. 5, color blue no. 32; steel crochet hooks no. 6 and 7 **or the size that will give you the correct gauge;** 2 pearl buttons ¼″ in diameter.
GAUGE: With no. 6 hook:

Edging: 4 (ch-2) loops = 1″; 1 scallop = 1″.

Slippers: 8 dc = 1″.

KIMONO

Enlarge pattern (see page 22). Each square equals 1″. For front cut 2 pieces, for back cut 1 piece on fold. With right sides together, stitch shoulder, underarm and side seams. Trim seams and clip underarm curves carefully.

Along front, neck, lower edges and wrists, fold raw edges ¼″ over to wrong side, then fold under ¼″ once more. Baste.

EDGING:

1st rnd: With right side of work facing you, start at right shoulder seam, using no. 7 hk. Work 1 hdc ¼″ below edge (ch 2, sk ¼″ of edge, hdc over edge) 271 times, ch 2, join with sl st to first hdc. (272 lps made—20 lps along back neck edge, 16 lps along each front neck edge, 52 along each front, 4 along each rounded lower front edge, and 108 lps along lower edge.)
2nd rnd: Change to no. 6 hk. * Ch 3, sk next lp, keeping last lp of each dc on hk, work 2 dc in next lp, y o, draw through all 3 lps on hk (joined dc made), ch 3, sc in 3rd ch from hk (p made), work another joined dc in same lp, ch 3, sk 1 lp, sc in next lp (1 scallop made). Rep from * around (68 scallops made). Join with sl st to base of first ch-3. Break off.
Wrist Edge: With right side facing you, using no. 7 hk, start with 1 hdc at underarm seam at wrist edge. Work in patt of (ch 2 and 1 hdc) 31 times around edge, ch 2, join with sl st to first hdc (32 lps made).

Rep 2nd rnd of edging on kimono (8 scallops made).

Remove all basting threads.
Ties: Using no. 6 hk, attach thread to first p below V neck on left front, ch 45 to measure about 5½″. Break off, leaving a 4″ end. Crochet a tie in the same manner in 4th and 7th p below V neck. Work opposite side to correspond (6 ties).
Tassels (6): Cut a piece of cardboard 1½″ x 3″. Wind thread 35 times around shortest side, sl thread from cardboard, tie one

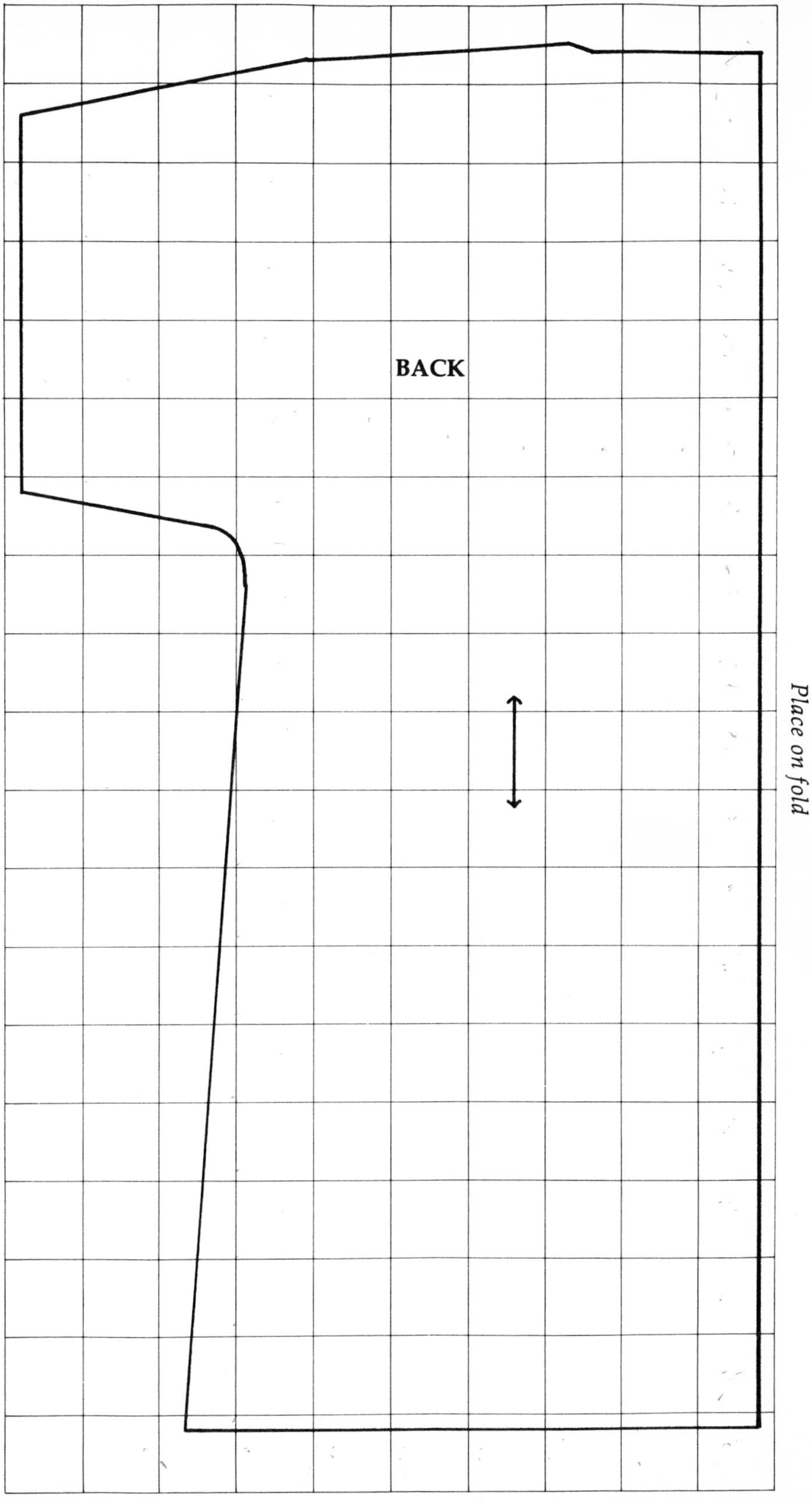

BACK

Place on fold

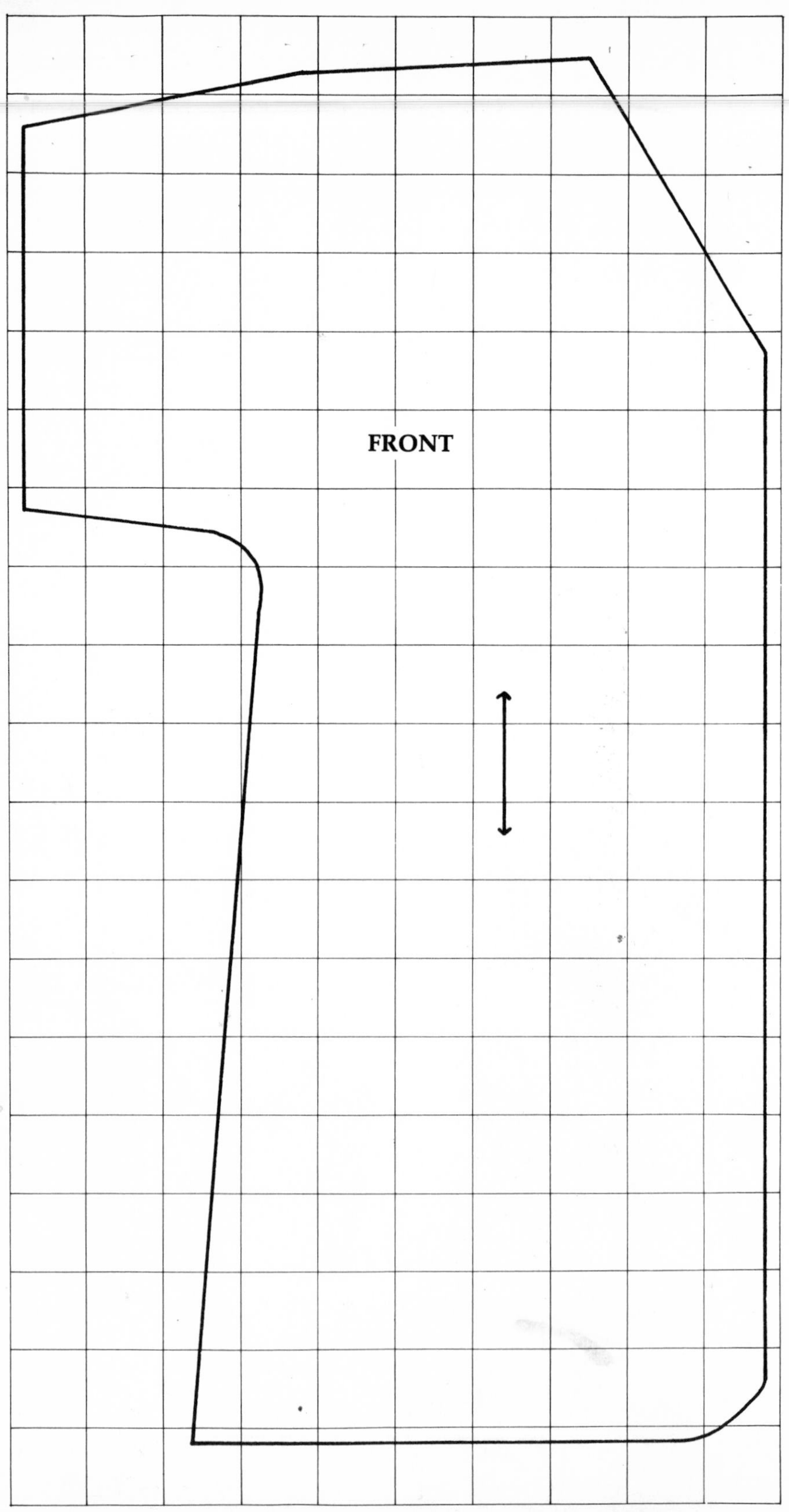
FRONT

end securely. Cut lps and trim ends. Attach 1 tassel to end of each tie.

SLIPPERS

RIGHT SLIPPER:

Sole: Starting at center, using no. 6 hk, ch 18.

1st rnd: Sc in 2nd ch and each ch across, working 3 sc in last ch. Do not turn, but continue along opposite side of foundation chain, work 1 sc in each of next 16 sts, work 3 sc in skipped ch-1 at beg of rnd (38 sc). Do not join.

2nd rnd: Ch 3, dc in same place as last sc, work 2 dc in next sc, dc in each of next 14 sc, 2 dc in each of next 2 sc, dc in next sc, 2 dc in each of next 2 sc, dc in each of next 14 sc, 2 dc in each of next 3 sc, join with sl st to top of first ch-3 (47 dc).

3rd rnd: Ch 3, dc in same place as last sl st, 2 dc in next sc, dc in each of next 17 dc, 2 dc in each of next 6 dc, dc in each of next 17 dc, 2 dc in each of next 3 dc, dc in next dc, 2 dc in last dc. Join with sl st to top of ch-3 (59 dc).

4th rnd: Sc in each dc around (59 sc). Do not join.

Side: 5th rnd: Ch 3, dc in next and each sc around, working in front lp of each st only (59 dc). Join with sl st to top of ch-3.

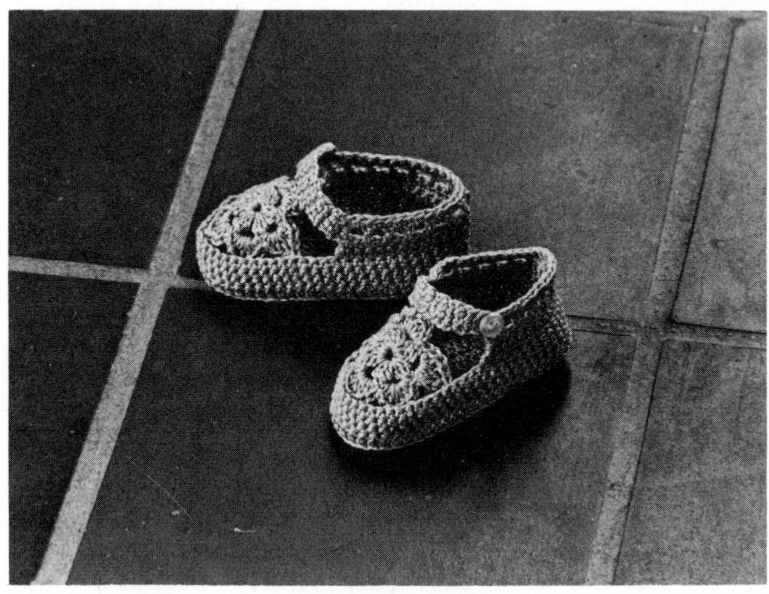

6th rnd: Marking beg of each rnd, sc in each st around. Do not join (59 sc).

Rep 6th rnd twice more.

Heel:

9th row: Sc in each of next 14 sc, ch 1, turn.

10th row: Sc in first and each of next 28 sc (29 sc). Ch 1, turn.

Rep 10th row twice more. Ch 4, turn at end of last row.

13th row: Skip next sc, dc in next sc, * ch 1, skip 1 sc, dc in next sc. Rep from * across. Ch 1, turn.

14th row: Sc in each dc and ch-1 sp across, ending with sc in top of turning ch. Do not turn or break off.

Strap: Work 3 sc over turning ch. Ch 1, turn.

Next row: Sc in first and each sc across. Ch 1, turn. Repeat last row until strap measures 1½". At end of last row, ch 5 for button lp. Join with sl st to beg of last row. Break off.

Along upper toe section 30 unworked sts remain. Starting at right-hand corner, mark 4th, 10th, 15th, 21st and 27th sc. Also mark center of lower strap edge.

Flower Motif (for toe section): Starting at center, ch 6. Join with sl st to form ring.

1st rnd: Ch 3, keeping last lp of each dc on hk, work 2 dc in ring, y o, draw through all lps on hk (3 dc-shell made, counting ch 3 as 1 dc), * ch 3, keeping last lp of each dc on hk, work 3 dc in ring, y o, draw through all 4 lps on hk, rep from * 4 times more, ch 3, join with sl st to top of first shell.

2nd rnd (joining rnd): * In next ch-3 lp, work 1 sc, 1 hdc and 2 dc, ch 1, drop lp from hk, insert hk in front lp of 1st marked st and pull dropped lp through (joining made), ch 1, work 2 dc, 1 hdc and 1 sc in same lp. Rep from * 5 times more, joining flower motif to remaining 4 marked sts and strap. Join with sl st to first sc. Break off.

LEFT SLIPPER: Work same as right slipper through 14th row. Break off. Work 3 sc over post of dc on right-hand corner of heel at beg of 13th row. Complete strap as before. Sew buttons in place.

SUNSUIT

For a fashion-conscious baby, these pants—in deep turquoise trimmed in scarlet and light purple—are worked in a simple but attractive pattern. It would serve equally well as a warm woolly suit in winter, when worn over a long-sleeved pullover and tights.

SHOWN IN COLOR

SIZE: 4–6 months. Pants measure about 20″ around middle when slightly stretched. Side seams measure 7¾″; from edge of bib to crotch, 10½″.
MATERIALS: Knitting worsted, 4 oz. deep turquoise, 1 oz. each scarlet and light purple; aluminum crochet hook size E **or the size that will give you the correct gauge;** 2 snaps.
GAUGE: 5 sts (1 sc, ch 1, 1 sc, ch 1, 1 sc) = 1″; 5 rows = 1″.
Note: Pants are made in one rectangular piece with one side seam. Starting at crotch edge with deep turquoise, ch 94 to measure about 19″.
1st row: Sc in 2nd ch from hk, * ch 1, sk 1 ch, sc in next ch. Rep from * across (47 sc, 46 ch-1). Ch 2, turn.
2nd row: Sk first sc, sc in ch-1 sp, * ch 1, sc in next sp. Rep from * across, ending with sc in turning ch. Ch 2, turn.

Rep 2nd row for patt, working even until piece measures 6½″ from beg, ending at waist edge. Omit last ch 2. Break off and turn work.

FRONT BIB: Sk first 8 sts, attach deep turquoise with sl st to next sc, ch 2, sc in first sp (ch 1, sc in next sp) 14 times, ch 2, turn.

Work even in patt over these 29 sts, until bib measures 2¼″.

STRAP: Sc in first sp, ch 1, sc in next sp, ch 2, turn. Work even over these 3 sts until strap measures 2″. Omit last ch 2. Break off.

Sk center 22 sts of bib, attach turquoise to next sc, ch 2, sc in next sp, ch 1, sc in turning ch. Ch 2, turn. Complete as for other strap.

BACK BIB: Sk 18 center sts along waist edge, attach turquoise to next sc, and complete as for front bib, making straps 2½" long instead of 2".

CROTCH: Sk first 20 sts at lower edge, attach turquoise with sl st to base of next sc, ch 2, sc in next sp (ch 1, sc in next sp), twice. Ch 2, turn.

Work even over these 5 sts until crotch measures 2". Omit last ch-2. Break off, leaving a 6" end.

FINISHING: Sew side seam. Sew free end of crotch to corresponding place in back.

Bib Edging: With right side of work facing you, work 1 row each with scarlet and purple in sc, ch-1 patt evenly around waist edge, bib and straps. Join with sl st to first sc.

LEG EDGING:

1st rnd: With turquoise, make lp on hk, with right side of work facing you, sc in base of any sc, work evenly in (ch 1, sc) patt around, ending with ch 1, join with sl st to first sc.

2nd rnd: Sl st in next sp, sc in same sp, continue in patt around, ending ch 1, join with sl st to first sc.

Rep 2nd rnd twice more. Break off.

5th rnd: With scarlet make lp on hk, with right side facing you, sc in any ch-1 sp, work in patt around, ending with ch 1, join with sl st to first sc. Break off.

With light purple, rep 5th rnd once more.

Sew snaps in place, one-half of snap to wrong side of front strap, other half to right side of back strap.

With scarlet and light purple, make a twisted cord 32" long, weave through sts 1" below waist edge. Tie in front.

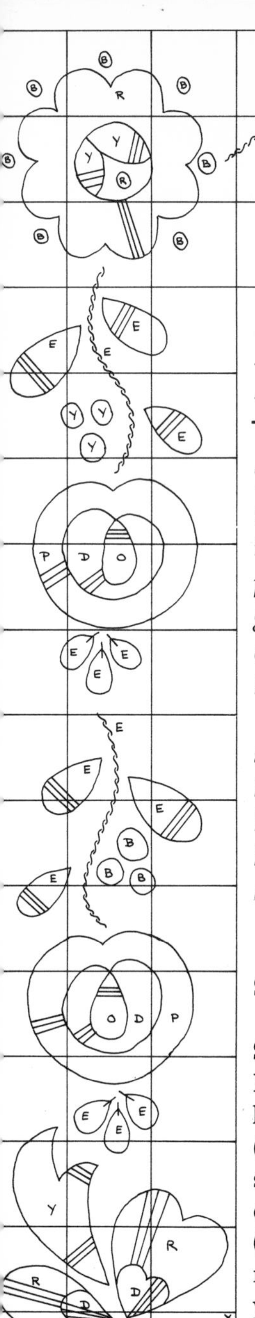

PEASANT BLANKET

This blanket is crocheted in single crochet, using a synthetic knitting worsted weight yarn. It is embroidered in the Hungarian folklore tradition with a red pineapple picot edging and bright-colored flowers against a dark green background. These flowers are worked in basic embroidery stitches—satin stitch, outline stitch, French knots and lazy daisy.

If you are not a crocheter and still have your heart set on making this blanket, work the embroidery on a loosely woven piece of woolen fabric. See how well knitting yarn works for the embroidery. If it is too heavy, try sport yarn or crewel yarn. Finish it off with a knotted fringe, tassels or a store-bought trim.

SHOWN IN COLOR

SIZE: 29″ x 34″, including edging.
MATERIALS: Bear Brand Win-Knit (100 percent orlon acrylic), 4 (4-oz.) skeins almond green no. 465, 1 (4-oz.) skein red no. 433; for embroidery, 1 oz. each synthetic knitting worsted weight yarn, yellow (Y), orange (O), pink (P), deep dusty rose (D), royal blue (B), emerald green (E), and red (R–no. 433); aluminum crochet hook size E **or the size that will give you the correct gauge;** 1 tapestry needle.
GAUGE: 9 sc = 1″; 6 rows = 1″.
CROCHET: With almond green ch 123 to measure about 27″.
1st row: Sc in 2nd ch from hk and in each ch across (122 sc). Ch 1, turn.
2nd row: Sc in first and each sc across. Ch 1, turn.

Rep 2nd row for patt until piece measures 32″ from beg. Omit last ch 1. Break off.

Pineapple Picot Edging: 1st rnd: With red make lp on hk, work in patt of sc, ch 1 evenly around all edges, skipping 2 sc on short sides and 2 rows on long sides. Work (sc, ch 1, sc, ch 1 and sc) in corners. Join with sl st to first sc.

2nd rnd: Sl st into first ch-1 sp, ch 2 (y o, pull up lp in ch 1 sp) twice, y o, pull through all 5 lps on hk—pineapple made. Ch 4, sl st in 3rd ch from hk (p made), * sk next sc, in next sp work (y o, pull up lp in ch 1 sp) 3 times, y o, draw through all 7 lps on (another pineapple made), p. Rep from * around, join with sl st to first ch of first p. Break off.

EMBROIDERY: Enlarge and trace pattern 4 times on tracing paper or tissue paper. Arrange tracings along outside edge of blanket about 3″ in from finished edging, to form a rectangular 3″-wide panel (place 2 tracings with right side up, 2 tracings with wrong side up, matching xs and ys).

Pin tracings to blanket and sew in place with needle and contrasting thread along all traced design lines. Carefully tear tracing away, leaving sewn stitches in place for outlines of embroidery.

Follow keys for colors and diagram for stitches. See page 153 on how to execute the stitches.

Embroider with a single strand of yarn, keeping tension even, especially when working satin stitch, so work won't pull up.

STITCH DIAGRAM

Satin stitch |||||

Stem stitch ~~~~~

French knot o

Lazy daisy ⊖-

T-SHIRT AND SOAKERS

This set is for the littlest ones, in an appealing combination of orchid and aqua baby yarn. The top is worked in one piece in a reversible half double crochet pattern and takes little yarn, with matching pants in the reverse color combination.

SHOWN IN COLOR

SIZE: Birth to 4 months. Shirt measures $8\frac{1}{2}''$ across at underarms and $8\frac{1}{4}''$ from shoulder to lower edge. Pants measure 20″ around middle, slightly stretched, and $8\frac{1}{4}''$ from waist to crotch.
MATERIALS: Baby or fingering yarn, for shirt: 2 (1-oz.) skeins orchid; for soakers: 2 (1-oz.) skeins aqua; aluminum crochet hook size B **or the size that will give you the correct gauge.**
GAUGE: 6 hdc = 1″; 5 hdc rows = 1″.

T-SHIRT

FRONT: Starting at lower edge with orchid, ch 53 loosely to measure $8\frac{1}{2}''$.
1st row: Hdc in 4th ch from hk and in each ch across (51 hdc—**note:** count turning ch as 1 hdc throughout). Ch 2, turn.
2nd row: Hdc in first hdc (ch 2 counts as first hdc), inserting hk under 3 top lps of each st, and each hdc across, hdc over turning ch. Ch 2, turn.

Rep 2nd row for patt 21 times more.

TO SHAPE FRONT OPENING AND SLEEVE:
1st row: Hdc in first and each of next 22 hdc (24 hdc). Do not work over remaining sts. Ch 2, turn.
***2nd row:** Hdc in first and each hdc across, hdc over turning ch (24 hdc), do not ch 2 and turn, but ch 15 for sleeve; turn.
3rd row: Hdc in 4th ch from hk and in each ch across (13 hdc),

then continue to work 1 hdc in each of next 23 hdc of front (36 hdc in all). Ch 2, turn.

Working across 36 hdc only, work 12 rows even in patt as established, ending at front opening. Ch 1, turn.

TO SHAPE NECK:
1st row: Sl st in first 11 hdc, ch 2, hdc in same sp as last sl st, and in each of next 24 hdc (26 hdc). Ch 2, turn.

Working across 26 hdc only, work 6 rows even in patt, ending at sleeve edge. * Omit ch 2 at end of last row. Break off.

Attach yarn with sl st to first hdc at beg of 23rd row (side edge). Ch 2, hdc in each of next 23 hdc (24 hdc), leaving center 3 hdc unworked. Ch 2, turn.

Complete in *same* manner as first half, repeating from * to *. Ch 2, turn at end of last row.

BACK:
1st row: Hdc in first and each of next 24 hdc, ch 23 for back neck, work 2 hdc in first hdc on corresponding row at opposite neck corner, hdc in each of next 24 hdc. Ch 2, turn.
2nd row: Hdc in first and each of next 24 hdc, hdc in each of next 23 sts, work 2 hdc in next hdc, hdc in each of next 24 hdc (75 hdc). Ch 2, turn.

Work 13 rows even in patt. At end of last row, ch 1, turn.
Next row: Sl st in first 13 hdc, ch 2, hdc in same place as last sl st and in each of next 49 hdc (51 hdc), leaving remaining sts unworked. Ch 2, turn.

Working over 51 hdc only, work 24 rows even in patt. Omit ch 2 at end of last row. Break off.

FINISHING: Sew underarm and side seams.

EDGING:
1st rnd: With orchid make lp on hk, with outside of work facing you, sc evenly around lower edge of shirt. Join with sl st to first sc. Break off.
2nd rnd: With aqua make lp on hk, sc in any sc of 1st rnd, * ch 3, sl st in 3rd ch from hk (p made), sk 1 sc, sc in next sc. Rep from * around. Join and break off.

Work edging in same manner around neck opening and sleeve edges.
Tie: with aqua make a chain 13″ long, thread through 2 corresponding ps at upper corners of front opening.

SOAKERS

Note: Soakers are worked in one rectangular piece with a side seam.

Starting at waist edge with aqua, ch 110 to measure about 18″. Work in patt as for shirt (108 hdc) until piece measures 6″ from beg. Omit last ch 2. Break off.

FRONT CROTCH:

1st row: Sk first 12 hdc on last row, attach aqua with sl st to next hdc, ch 3, hdc in each of next 29 sts (30 hdc, counting ch 3 as 1 hdc). Ch 2, turn.

2nd (dec) row: Work in patt across, dec 1 hdc at beg and end of row and 2 hdc evenly spaced in between. Dec 1 hdc as follows: y o, pull up 1 lp in each of next 2 sts, y o, draw through all 5 lps on hk—26 hdc). Ch 2, turn.

3rd row: Work even. Ch 2, turn.

Rep 2nd and 3rd rows once more (22 hdc).

6th (dec) row: Working in patt across, dec 1 hdc at beg, center and end of row (19 hdc). Ch 2, turn.

Work even on 19 hdc until crotch measures 2¼″. Omit ch 2. Break off.

BACK CROTCH:

1st row: Sk 24 center hdc on lower edge of pants section, attach aqua with sl st to next hdc and complete as for front section.

FINISHING: Sew side and crotch seams.

Edging: Work 1 rnd sc each with aqua and orchid evenly around waist edge and leg openings. With orchid make a chain 28″ long. Weave through 2nd row below waist and tie in front.

YELLOW JACKET AND BONNET

This bright jacket was inspired by the coats worn by fishermen on the Greek island of Crete.

SHOWN IN COLOR

The technique of finishing the edges of fabric pieces with crochet and then joining them with crochet is attractively simple and can be applied to many projects. The sketches of the bunting, jumper and kimono will give you some additional ideas. (See page 51.)

To poke small holes in the fabric to be crocheted around, a fine crochet hook is used at first. When working the remaining crochet, you can either change to a larger hook more in proportion to the weight of yarn being used, or you can continue with the same fine hook, but work more loosely—whatever is more comfortable.

Specific directions are given for this particular jacket and bonnet. However, you may wish to create your own design or adapt something from an existing commercial pattern, using this joining method.

When using a commercial pattern, omit all seam allowances on the pattern and cut out pieces on the sewing lines. In both cases, it is a good idea to make a sample swatch with the yarn, hook and fabric you are planning to use to get an idea of their proportion to each other. This swatch will show you how much the crocheted edges and joining row will add to the size of a pattern piece. For example, if two finished edges and a joining row measure ½″ wide, cut each edge ¼″ smaller.

It is advisable to use a fabric that doesn't fray easily. Bonded fabrics, knits, fake fur and pile fabrics are suitable, as well as cottons, flannels and woolens.

If you have a piece of fabric at hand that does fray too much, but you want to use it anyway, add 1/4" hem allowance around all pieces. Turn under all raw edges 1/4" and baste in place; remove basting thread when garment is completed.

SIZE: 6–12 months. Jacket measures 24" around chest and 6" from armhole to lower edge. Sleeve length is 6 1/4".
MATERIALS: 3/4 yd. of 36"-wide medium-weight yellow wool fabric; small amounts of orange and yellow knitting worsted and shocking pink sport yarn; aluminum crochet hooks, sizes B and E.

Enlarge patterns (see page 22). Each square equals 1 square inch. Place pattern pieces on straight vertical grain of fabric. For back of jacket, cut 1 piece on fold; for front, cut 2 pieces, reversing 1; for sleeves, cut 4 pieces, reversing 2; for bonnet, cut 2 side sections, reversing 1, and 1 center section. Do not add any seam allowances.

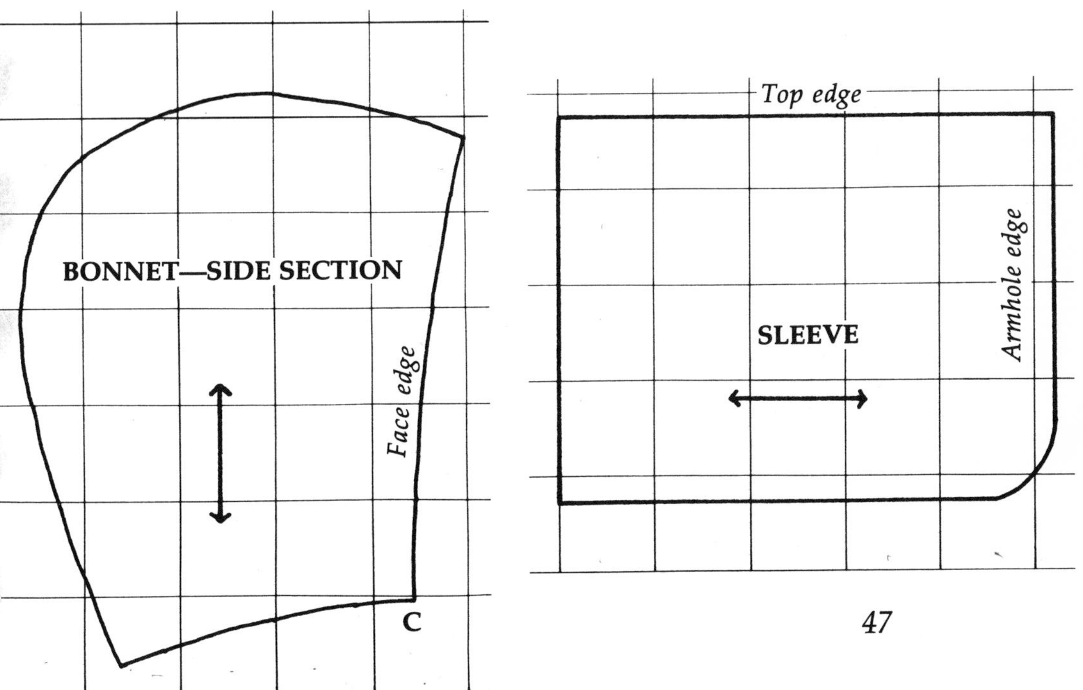

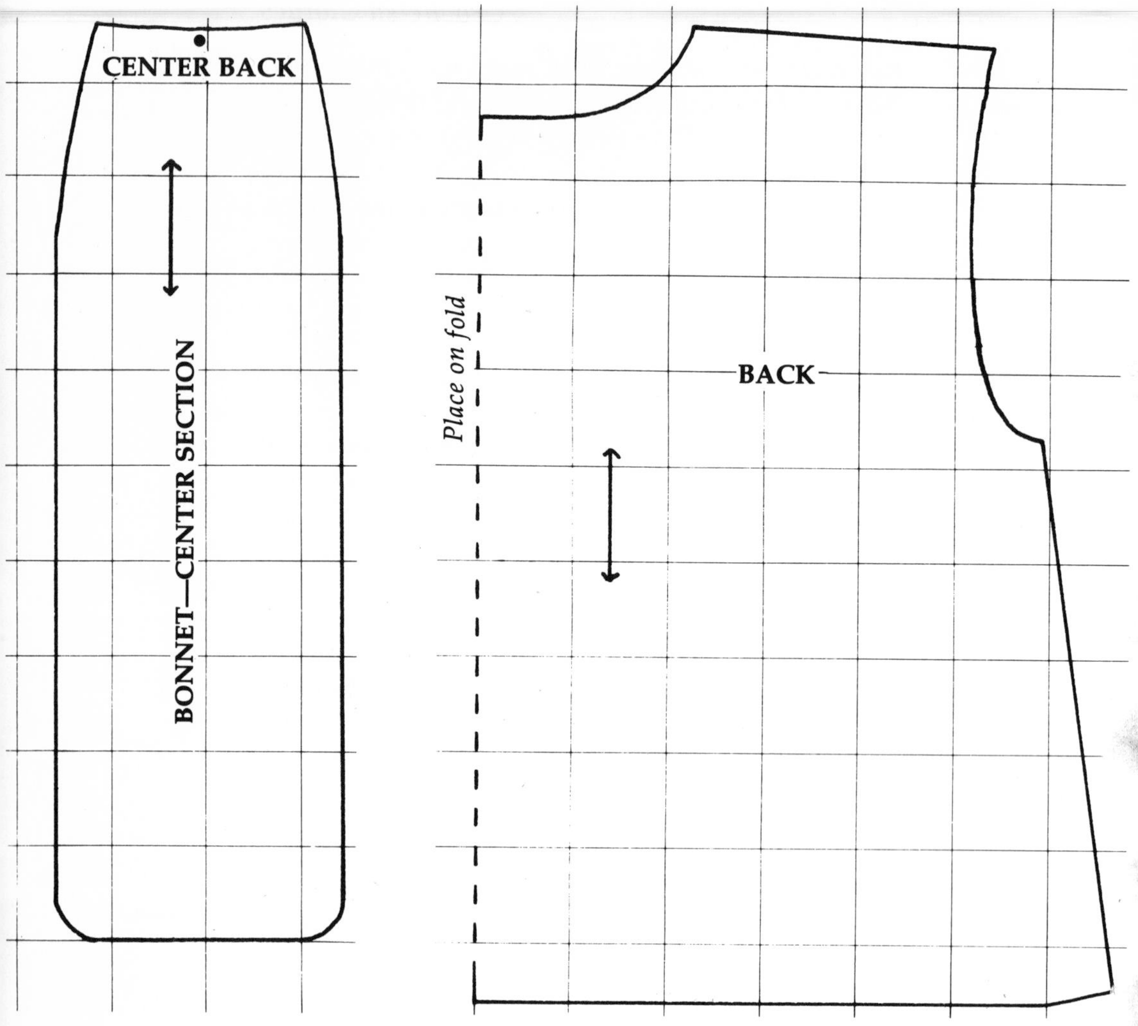

JACKET

CROCHET EDGING: With size B hk and orange make lp on hk, sc over 3/8″ of edge, * ch 1, sk 3/8″ of edge, sc over 3/8″ of edge. Rep from * around all edges of all pieces, working 3 sc in corners. Join with sl st to first sc. Break off.

TO ASSEMBLE—JOINING ROW: Change to size E hk. Crochet left front to back as follows: With right side of front facing you, attach shocking pink with sl st to top lp of first sc at shoulder corner A on patt, ch 1, working in top lp of each st

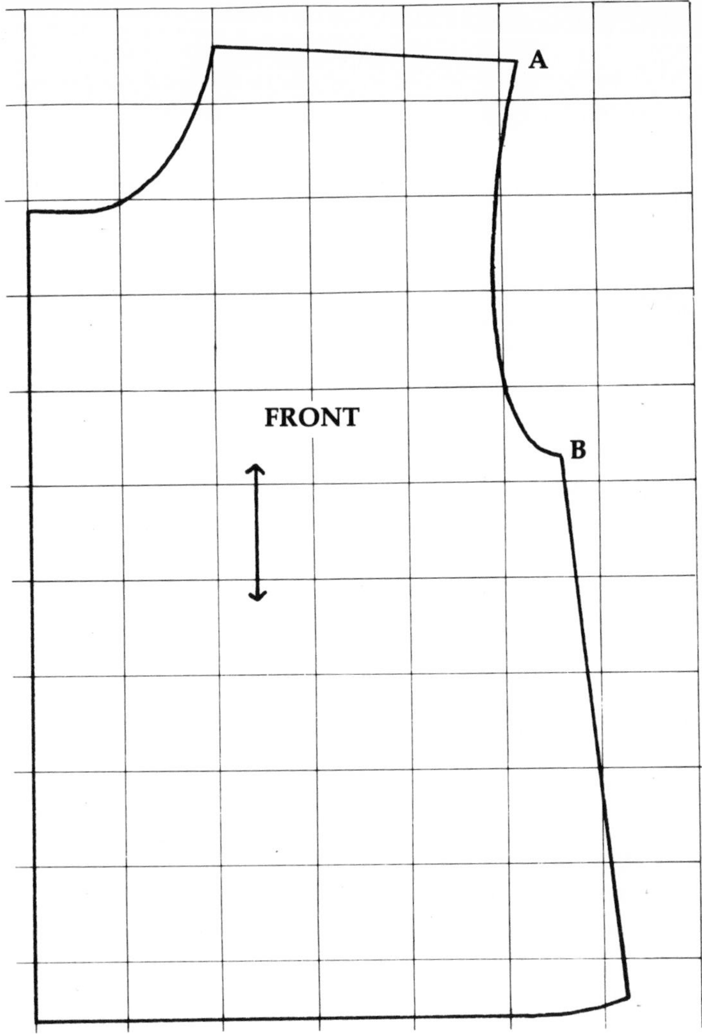

only, sl st in corresponding st at shoulder corner of back, * ch 1, sk 1 st on front shoulder, sl st in next st, ch 1, sk 1 st on back shoulder, sl st in next st. Repeat from * across shoulder. Break off.

Join right front to back in same manner, starting at neck corner of right front. Join top edges of sleeve sections and side sections of bonnet to center section in same manner.

Crochet left sleeve to jacket as follows: Attach shocking pink with sl st to top lp of first sc at armhole corner B on left front, ch 1, sl st in sleeve corner. Continue in patt, joining sleeve to jacket, matching joining rows of shoulder and sleeve. Join right sleeve in same manner, starting at armhole corner on back.

Join fronts to back as before along side and underarm edges.

FINISHING:

Jacket: Border for neck, front and lower edge: With right side of work facing you, attach shocking pink with sl st to top lp of any st at center back neck, ch 2, working in top lp of each st only, hdc in each st around, working 3 hdc in corners at front neck and lower front, join with sl st to top of first ch 2. Break off.

Ties: Make 6. Mark each front edge for 3 ties, the first one 1/4" below neck edge, the others each 2 1/2" apart. Attach shocking pink with sl st to top of hdc at marker. Ch 40, sl st in 2nd ch from hk and each ch across, sl st in next hdc. Break off. Weave in ends. Work 5 more ties in this manner.

Cuffs: Note: All rnds are worked with right side of work facing you.

1st rnd: Attach orange with sl st to any one st at wrist edge, using size E hk, ch 2, working in top lp of each st only, work 43 hdc evenly around (44 hdc, counting first ch 2 as first hdc). Join with sl st to top of ch 2. Break off.

2nd rnd: With yellow, make lp on hk, sc in any 1 hdc, sc in each of next 43 hdc around. Join with sl st (44 sc). Break off.

3rd rnd: Attach shocking pink to any 1 sc, ch 3, work 3 hdc in same sp, drop lp from hk, insert hk into top of ch 3, draw dropped lp through, ch 1 to fasten (popcorn made), * sk 1 sc, work 4 hdc in next sc, drop lp from hk, insert hk in top of first hdc of 4-hdc group, pull dropped lp through, ch 1 to fasten (2nd popcorn made). Rep from * 20 times more. Ch 1, sk 1 sc, join to top of first popcorn (22 popcorns made in all). Break off.

4th rnd: With yellow, make lp on hk, sc in any ch-1 sp, * ch 1, sc in next ch-1 sp. Rep from * around. Ch 1, join with sl st (44 sts). Break off.

5th rnd: Attach orange with sl st to any 1 st, ch 2, hdc in each st around. Join with sl st to top of ch 2 (44 hdc). Break off.

P rnd: With shocking pink, make lp on hk, sc in any 1 sc and each of next 3 sc, * ch 3, sl st in 3rd ch from hk (p made), sc in each of next 4 sc. Rep from * around. Join. Break off.

BONNET

FACE AND NECK BORDER: Note: all rows wre worked with right side of work facing you.

1st row: With yellow, make lp on hk, sc in first sc at side section corner C on pattern. Work 76 sc evenly across face edge (77 sc in all). Break off.

2nd row: Attach shocking pink with sl st to first sc, ch 3, work 4 hdc popcorn in next sc, * sk 1 sc, work popcorn in next sc. Rep from * across, ch 3, sl st in last sc (38 popcorns). Break off.

3rd row: With yellow, make lp on hk, sc in top of first ch-3, * ch 1, sc in next ch-1 sp. Rep from * across, ending with sc in top of last ch-3. Break off.

Last rnd: With orange, make lp on hk, sc in first sc and each st across face edge, ch 3, do not break off, but continue to hdc evenly along neck edge. Join with sl st to first sc. Break off.

Cord: With shocking pink, make a chain 25″ long. Sl st in 2nd ch from hk and each ch across. Break off.

Weave cord through hdcs at neck edge. Make a knot at each end of cord.

BASSINET SET—2 Sheets and 1 Pillowcase

With the country-fresh look of gingham and filet crochet, this old-fashioned lacy crochet has made a recent comeback. It is versatile and easy to make. Once you have mastered the technique, you can make your own designs.

Filet crochet consists of blocks and spaces. Designs are charted out on graph paper the same way you would a cross-stitch or needlepoint design, where each square equals 1 stitch.

If you feel a bit timid about tackling filet crochet, add the pretty edging that was used on the Baby Blue Kimono on page 33. Be careful when working this edging in rows instead of rounds; you'll need a multiple of 4 loops plus 1 loop to complete the scallop pattern (see page 20 for an explanation of the term "multiple"). You could even use cotton flannel for the sheets and pillowcase if yours is a winter baby.

If you want to make something really quickly, instead of crocheting the trim, finish off a gingham set with a pretty white ruffled eyelet border about 2" wide.

As you see, there are many variations, and either way you'll have an attractive set.

SHOWN IN COLOR

SIZES: Sheets 27" x 40", without edging; pillowcase 11½" x 16⅙", without edging; edging 2" wide; length is adjustable.
MATERIALS: J. & P. Coats "Knit-Cro-Sheen," 2 (175-yd.) balls red no. 126 (or Coats and Clark's Pearl Cotton no. 5, 7 (50-yd.) balls); steel crochet hook no. 7; 2 yds. of 45"-wide red gingham.

GAUGE: 5 sps and 4 rows = 1″.

SHEETS

Cut 2 gingham rectangles 28″ x 41″. This includes a ¼″ hem. Turn under ¼″ all around, then turn folded edges ¼″ to wrong side. Pin or baste. Stitch in place.

PILLOWCASE

Cut 2 gingham rectangles 12″ x 17¼″. This allows for a ¼″ seam along 3 sides and a ¼″ hem along 1 side.

Turn under ¼″ on 1 narrow end of each rectangle. Then turn folded edge ¼″ to wrong side. Pin or baste. Stitch in place.

With right sides together, matching hemmed edges, pin pieces together. Stitch 3 sides, leaving hemmed side open. Turn right side out.

SHEET EDGING: Starting at narrow end, ch 22.
1st row: Work double dc (dbl dc) in 5th ch from hk as follows: y o, pull up a lp in ch, y o and draw through 2 lps on hk, y o and pull up lp in same ch, y o and draw through 2 lps on hk, y o and draw through all 3 lps on hk (dbl dc made); dc in next ch (bl made); ch 1, sk 1 ch, dc in next ch (sp made); work (1 bl, 1 sp) 3 times; then 1 bl. Ch 4, turn.
2nd row: Sk first dc and dbl dc, dc in next dc (sp over bl); ch 1, dc in next dc (sp over sp); ch 1, sk dbl dc, dc in next dc (sp over bl); work 5 more sps, ch 1, dc in top of turning ch. Ch 3, turn.
3rd row: Work dbl dc in first sp, dc in next dc (bl over sp); work 7 sps, dbl dc in next sp, dc in 3rd ch of turning ch-4. Ch 4, turn.
Starting with 4th row, follow chart to B, then repeat from A to B 10 times more (22 flower motifs in all).

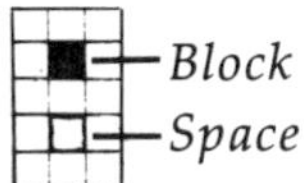

FILET CROCHET CHART

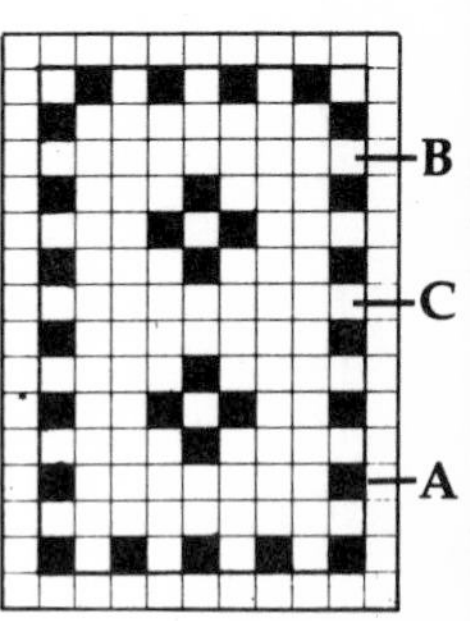

Next row: Work 1 bl, 7 sps, 1 bl. Ch 4, turn.
Following row: Work 1 sp (1 bl, 1 sp) 4 times. Omit ch-3. Do not turn or break off, but continue to work across long side.
Trim: Sc over end st of first row (a sp). Ch 3, sc in 3rd ch from hk (p made), sc over end of same row, * ch 5, sk next row (a bl); (sc, p, sc) over end st of next row (a sp).
Rep from * across, ending with ch 5, sk bl, sc in end stitch of next row (a bl). Break off.

PILLOW EDGING: Starting at narrow end, ch 22.
1st row: Working in same manner as sheet edging, work 1 bl, 7 sps, 1 bl. Ch 4, turn.
2nd row: Work 9 sps across. Ch 3, turn.
Starting with a 3rd row, follow chart to B, then rep from A to B 8 times more, then rep from A to C once more (19 flower motifs in all). Omit last ch 3. Do not turn or break off, but work trim as for sheet.
FINISHING: Sew edging to right side of narrow end of 1 sheet, and around outside hemmed opening of pillowcase. Sew narrow ends together.

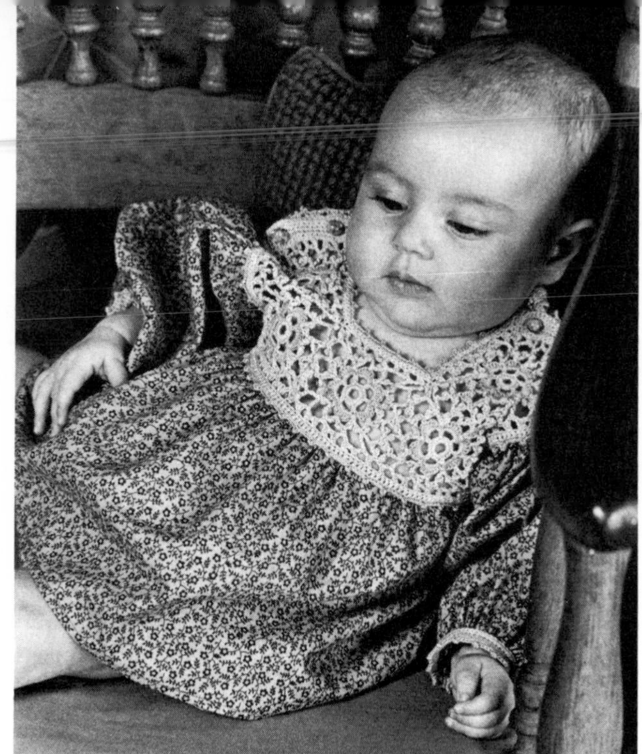

IRISH LACE
FOR LITTLE GIRLS

The Irish lace bonnet and yoke on the calico dress on the following pages are not really a "lace" at all, but a delicate and airy method of crochet.

The calico dress has a two-tone crocheted yoke, which is worked in squares that are joined together as you go along. These squares are in the accent color of the dress fabric. The yoke buttons at the shoulders. Gathered rectangles of fabric are sewn together to form the "body" of the dress. Matching bloomers complete the set.

The most practical way to put this dress on the baby is to unbutton the shoulders and lower the baby into the dress, rather than pulling it over the head.

If you work the yoke completely in white and make a long skirt section of white batiste, a fine handkerchief

linen or organdy, it will make a lovely christening dress. In which case, cut the skirt 26" long instead of 7¾". You'll need 2 yds. of 45"-wide fabric for the long version.

The charmingly old-fashioned granny bonnet is worked in the traditional picot loops of Irish crochet. The bonnet has a 3-layer rose motif topping the crown and could not be simpler to make. It is only a slightly ruffled circle, gathered to fit with a narrow velvet or satin ribbon. Almost any pretty doily 12" in diameter could be turned into such a lovely headdress. Cotton thread was used for both yoke and bonnet.

Irish crochet originated as recently as the mid-nineteenth century in an Ursuline convent in Cork, where the nuns taught crochet lacemaking to the children.

This crocheted "lace," worked with special, very thin thread and hair-fine hooks, originally imitated the priceless laces of fifteenth-century France and Italy. But in time it became a work of art in its own right. What began as a poor woman's lace eventually became popular in the most fashionable and aristocratic circles, and later developed into a national cottage industry.

IRISH LACE YOKE DRESS AND BLOOMERS

SIZE: 2–6 months. Dress measures 10½″ across back at underarms, 12″ from shoulder to lower edge. Sleeve length is 6½″. Bloomers measure 9½″ from waist to crotch and 26″ around waist (stretched). Dress buttons at the shoulders.
MATERIALS: 1 yd. of 36″-wide purple and aqua calico printed cotton for dress and bloomers; for yoke and wrist edgings: J. & P. Coats "Knit-Cro-Sheen," 2 (175-yd.) balls aqua no. 76 and 1 ball lavender no. 37; steel crochet hook no. 9 **or the size that will give you the correct gauge;** 1¼ yds. round elastic; 4 ball buttons ⅜″ in diameter.
GAUGE: Yoke: Each square measures 2¼″.

YOKE—FRONT:
1st Square: Note: Work tightly for best results. Starting at center of flower with aqua, ch 8. Join with sl st to form ring. Right side of work is always facing you.
1st rnd: Ch 1, work 18 sc in ring. Join with sl st to first sc.
2nd rnd: Sc in same place as sl st, * ch 5, sk next 2 sc, sc in next sc. Rep from * around, ending last rep with sl st in first sc (6 lps made). Break off.
3rd rnd: Attach lavender with sl st to any ch-5 lp, in each lp work 1 sc, 1 hdc, 5 dc, l hdc, 1 sc (6 petals made). Join with sl st to first sc. Break off.
4th rnd: Attach aqua with sl st to sp between any 2 petals. * (ch 5, sc in 4th ch from hk) twice, ch 1 (dpl made), sc in center dc of next petal, work dpl, sc between next 2 petals. Rep from * around. Join with sl st to first sl st (12 dpl made).
5th rnd: Sl st to center of next dpl, ch 3, work dpl, tr in same place as last sl st (first corner lp made), * (work dpl, sc between ps of next dpl) twice, work 1 dpl, between p of next dpl work 1 tr, 1 dpl and 1 tr (another corner lp made). Rep from * 3 times more, ending last rep with 1 dpl, join with sl st to 3rd ch of first ch-3. Break off.
2nd Square: Work same as for first square through 4th rnd.
5th Joining rnd: Sl st to center of next dpl, ch 8, p, join with sl st between p of a corner lp on first square, ch 5, p, ch 1, tr in base of ch-8 on 2nd square (joining completed—1 corner lp of each square joined), * ch 5, p, sl st between p of next dpl on first square, ch 5, p, ch 1, sl st between p of next dpl on 2nd square. Rep from * once more. Ch 5, p, sl st between p of next

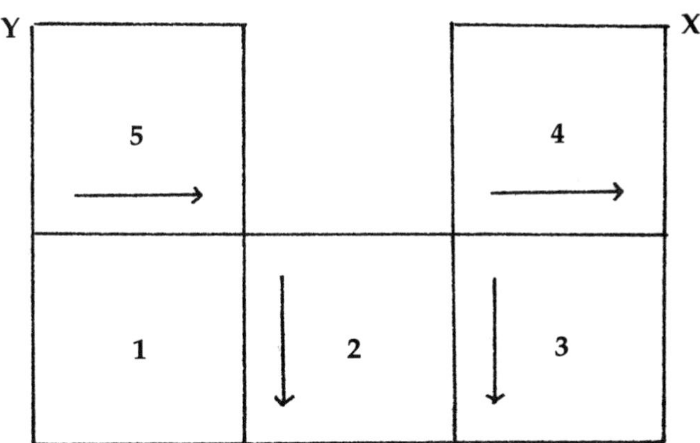

dpl on first square, ch 5, p, ch 1, tr between p of next dpl on 2nd square, ch 5, p, sl st between p of next corner lp on first square, ch 5, p, ch 1, tr in same place as last tr on 2nd square (1 side joined). Complete rnd by repeating from * on 5th rnd of first square on last 3 sides, ending with sl st in 3rd ch of ch-8. Break off.

Work squares 3, 4 and 5 in same manner. Following diagram, join 3rd square to 2nd square, 4th to 3rd, 5th to first square as before, in the direction of the arrows.

YOKE—BACK: Work same as for front.

Front Yoke Edging: 1st row: With aqua, make lp in hk, with right side of work facing you, sc in center st of corner lp (X on diagram), sc in next p, * (ch 2, sc in next p, ch 1, sc in next p) 3 times, ch 2, sc in next p, sc in center st of next corner lp (21 sts). Ch 1, turn.

2nd row: Working in top lp of each st, sc in first and each st across (21 sc). Ch 1, turn.

Working through both lps of each st, rep 2nd row 3 times more, ending at neck edge, ch 1, continue along inner left neck edge, sc inside of each of next 4 sc rows, ch 1, sc in next p (of corner lp), * (ch 2, sc in next p, ch 1, sc in next p) * 3 times, ch 2, sc in next p (of corner lp), ch 1, sc in corner, work along inner front neck edge, ch 1, sc in next p (of next corner lp). Rep from * to * 3 times, ch 2, sc in p of corner lp, ch 1, sc in corner, continue along inner right neck edge, ch 1, sc in next p of next corner lp. Rep from * to * 3 times, ch 2, sc in next p (of corner lp), ch 1, in center st of same corner lp work 1 sc, ch 1 and 1 sc, continue across right shoulder edge, sc in next p (of corner lp). Rep from * to * 3 times, ch 2, sc in next p, sc in center st of corner lp, ch 1, turn.

Working across 21 sts of shoulder edge only, work 4 sc rows even, ch 1 to turn, ending at armhole edge. Do not turn, but continue along outer right-hand edge of yoke as follows: Sc inside of each of next 4 sc rows, ch 1, sc in next p. Rep from * to * 3 times, (ch 2, sc in next p) twice, rep from * to * 3 times, ch 2, sc in next p, ch 1, in center st of next corner lp, work 1 sc, ch 1 and 1 sc, continue along lower edge of yoke, ch 1, sc in next p. Rep from * to * 3 times, (ch 2, sc in next p) twice, rep from * to * 3 times, (ch 2, sc in next p) twice, rep from * to * 3 times, ch 2, sc in next p, ch 1, in center st of next corner lp, work 1 sc, ch 1 and 1 sc, continuing along outer left-hand edge of yoke, ch 1, sc in next p, rep from * to * 3 times, (ch 2, sc in next p) twice, repeat from * to * 3 times, ch 2, sc in next p, ch 1, sc inside of each of next 4 sc rows. Break off.

Next row: With wrong side of work facing you, attach aqua with sl st at Y on diagram, working in top lp of each st, sc in each st across right shoulder edge, ch 1, continue to sc in each st around neck edge, ch 1, and across left shoulder edge. Break off.

Back Yoke Edging: Work same as front edging, working 2 buttonholes on each shoulder edge as follows: Rep 2nd row once more instead of 3 times.

Buttonhole row: Sc in each of first 3 sc, ch 3, sk 3 sc, sc in each of next 9 sc, ch 3, sk 3 sc, sc in next sc and each of next 2 sc. Ch 1, turn.

5th row: Sc in each sc and ch across. Break off.

Sew buttons in place and button yoke.

Outer Yoke Edging: With wrong side of yoke facing you, attach aqua with sl st to lower back yoke edge, working in top lp of each st only, sc in each st around, working 1 sc, ch 1 and 1 sc in each corner and working through both layers at shoulder edge.

Picot Edge: With lavender, make lp on hk, starting at lower back yoke edge, with right side of work facing you, * sc in each of next 4 sc, ch 3, sl st in 3rd ch from hk (p made). Rep from * around. Join and break off.

Unbutton yoke and work p edge evenly along inner neck edge of both front and back yoke.

Cuffs (Make 2): With aqua, make a chain 5½″ long, being careful not to twist chain, join with sl st to first ch to form ring.

1st rnd: Ch 1, sc in next and each st around. Join with sl st to first sc.

Repeat 1st rnd once more. Break off.

With lavender, make lp on hk, sc around last aqua rnd made. Join and break off. With lavender work p edge around base of aqua rnd.

TO ASSEMBLE DRESS AND BLOOMERS:

For Skirt: Cut 2 rectangles 7¾″ x 17″ each.

Gather one long edge of each rectangle to measure 11″, leaving 1½″ at both ends ungathered (see diagram).

For Sleeves: Cut 2 rectangles 8¼″ x 17″ each. Gather 1 long edge of each rectangle to measure 10″, leaving 2¼″ at both ends ungathered (see diagram).

¼″ seam allowance is included in pattern.

With right sides of fabric together, sew 2 sleeve sections to one skirt section, following diagram between dots.

Sew second skirt section to sleeves in same manner. Clip at Vs, turn right side out.

Pin crocheted yoke over center neck opening, wrong side of yoke facing right side of dress. With small backstitches, sew yoke in place along outer edges of yoke, matching shoulder edges of yoke to Xs on sleeves (see diagram).

Fold dress in half crosswise and stitch underarm and side seams.

Turn lower edge of skirt ¼″ under to wrong side, fold again ¼″ under and stitch in place.

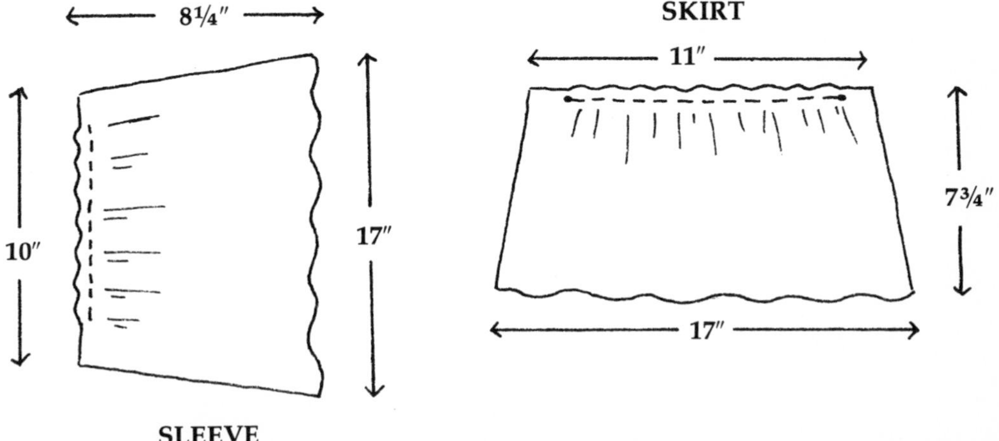

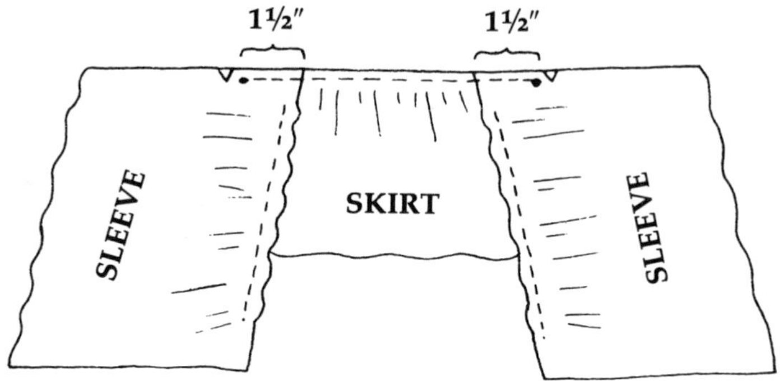

Turn sleeve edges ¼″ to wrong side and gather to measure about 5½″.

Sew crocheted cuffs over wrist edges with wrong side of cuff facing right side of sleeve.

Bloomers: Enlarge pattern (see page 22). Cut 1 piece each on fold for front and back.

With right sides together, sew side seams and crotch seam.

For casing, fold over ¾″ at waist edge to wrong side. Turn raw edge under ¼″ and stitch casing in place, leaving an opening to insert elastic.

Make a casing around each leg opening in same manner.

Cut elastic to fit around waist and leg and run through casings. Sew ends together securely.

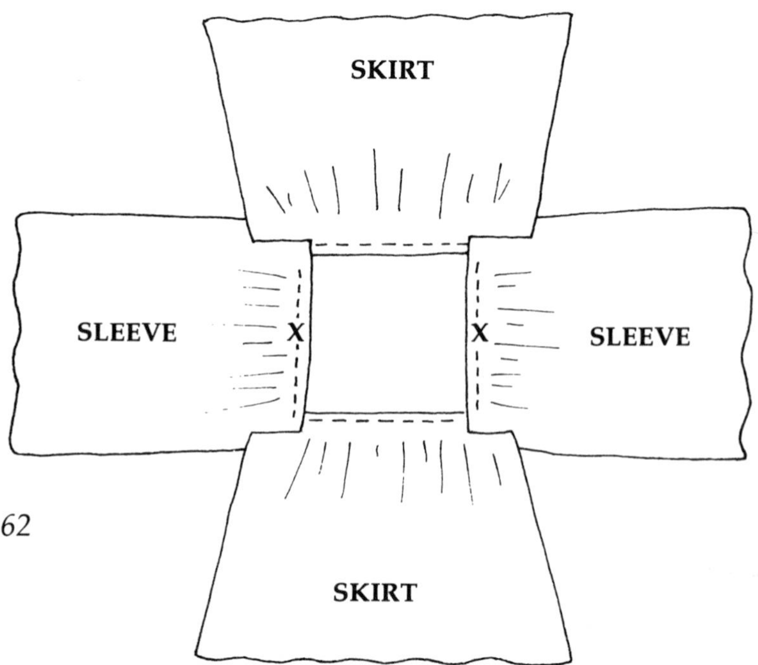

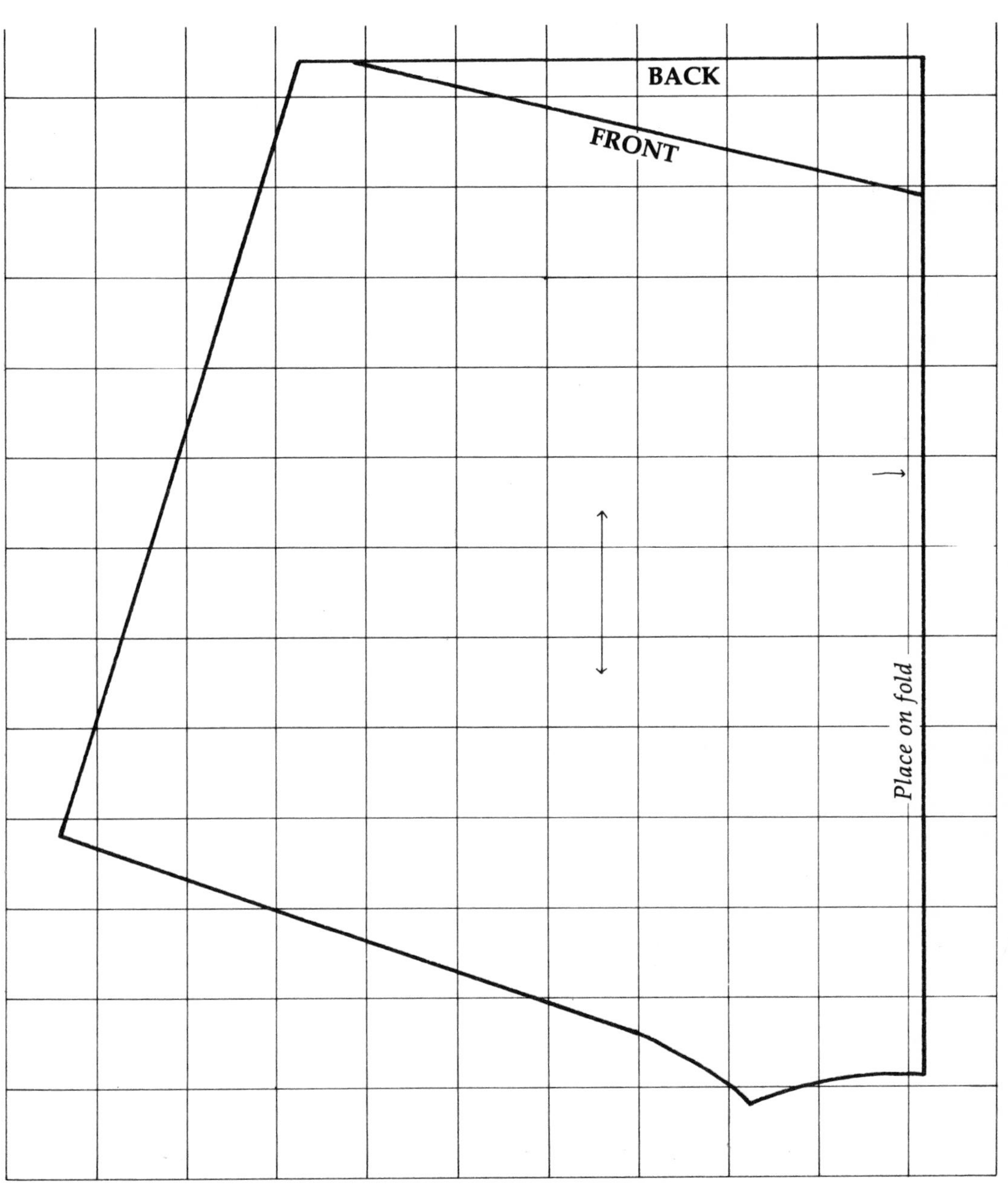
BACK
FRONT
Place on fold

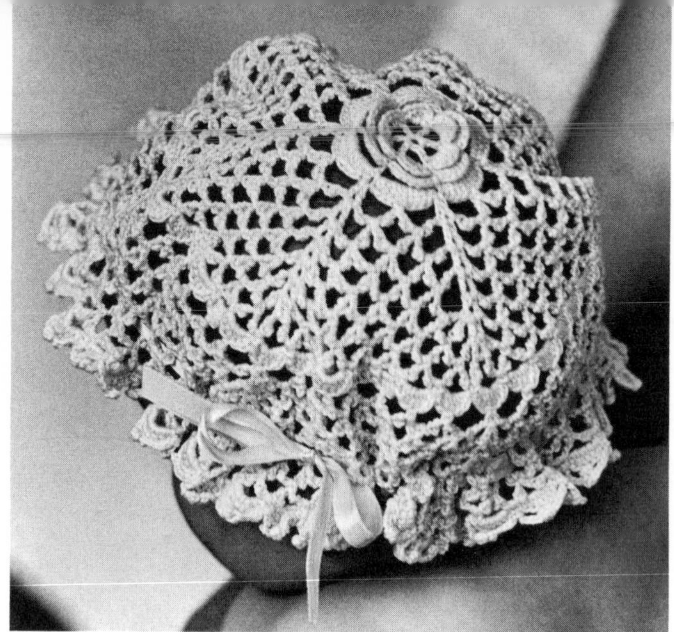

IRISH LACE BONNET

SIZE: Infant. Bonnet is worked in a circle 12″ in diameter.
MATERIALS: 1 (250-yd.) ball J. & P. Coats "Knit-Cro-Sheen" ecru no. 61; steel crochet hook no. 6 **or the size that will give you the correct gauge;** 1 yd. ¼″-wide satin or velvet ribbon.

GAUGE: 2 dpls = 1″; 3 dpl rnds = 1″.

Starting at top of crown, ch 5. Join with sl st to form ring.
1st rnd: Ch 6, dc in ring (mark dc with pin), (ch 3, dc in ring) 4 times, ch 3, join with sl st to 3rd ch of ch 6 (6 sps made).
2nd rnd: In each lp, work 1 sc, 1 hdc, 3 dc, 1 hdc, 1 sc. Join with sl st to first sc (6 petals made).
3rd rnd: Ch 5, sl st in back of work in next marked dc of first rnd (6 lps made across back of petals).
4th rnd: In each lp, work 1 sc, 1 hdc, 5 dc, 1 hdc and 1 sc, join with sl st to first sc (6 petals made behind first layer of petals).
5th rnd: * Ch 7, sl st in back of work in last sc of next petal. Rep from * around (6 lps made across back of petals).
6th rnd: In each lp, work 1 sc, 1 hdc, 7 dc, 1 hdc, 1 sc. Join with sl st to first sc (6 petals made behind 2nd layer of petals). Rose motif should measure 2″ in diameter.
7th rnd: Ch 4, dc in same place as last sl st * make a dpl as follows: ch 4, sc in 3rd ch from hk (p made), ch 4, p, ch 1 (dpl completed), sc in center dc of next petal, dpl, work 1 dc, ch 1, 1 dc-shell in sp between next 2 petals. Rep from * around, end-

ing last rep with dpl, join with sl st to 3rd ch of ch-4 (2 dpls between shells).

8th rnd: Sl st in ch-1 sp of first shell, ch 4, dc in same sp, * (dpl, sc between p of next lp) twice, dpl, shell in ch-1 sp of next shell. Rep from * around, ending last rep with dpl, join with sl st to 3rd ch of ch-4 (3 dpls between shells).

9th rnd: Sl st in ch-1 sp of first shell, ch 4, dc in same sp, * (dpl, sc between p of next lp) 3 times, dpl, shell in next shell. Rep from * around, ending last rep with dpl, join with sl st to 3rd ch of ch-4 (4 dpls between shells).

Rep 9th rnd for patt, 4 times more, working 1 more dpl between shells on each rnd (8 dpls between shells).

14th rnd: Turn work, sl st to center of last dpl made on previous rnd, turn (right side of work facing you again), ch 4, sk shell, sc between p of next dpl, * ch 4, sc between p of next dpl. Rep from * around, skipping shells (48 lps). Join with sl st.

15th rnd: In each ch-4 lp, work 1 sl st, 1 hdc, 5 dc, 1 hdc, 1 sl st (48 petals made). Join with sl st to first sl st.

16th rnd: Sl st to center dc of next petal, ch 2, sc in same place as last sl st, * (dpl, sc in center of next petal) 7 times, dpl, 1 sc, ch 1, 1 sc-shell in center of next petal. Rep from * around, ending last rep with dpl, join with sl st to first ch of ch-2 (8 dpls between shells).

17th rnd: Sl st in ch-1 sp of next shell, ch 4, dc in same sp, (dpl, sc between p of next dpl) 8 times, dpl, work 1 dc, ch 1, 1 dc-shell in next ch-1 sp. Rep from * around, ending last rep with dpl, sl st in 3rd ch of ch-4 (9 dpls between shells).

Rep 17th rnd for pattern 5 times more, working 1 more dpl between shells on each rnd (14 dpls between shells).

23rd rnd: Rep 14th rnd, working a ch-5 lp instead of a ch-4 lp (84 lps).

24th rnd: Rep 15 rnd (84 petals).

Edging: * Ch 5, in center dc of next petal, work 1 dc, ch 3, sc in 3rd ch from hk for p and 1 dc, ch 5, sl st in sp between next 2 petals. Rep from * around. Break off.

Weave ribbon through loops on 20th rnd, gather to fit and tie in a bow.

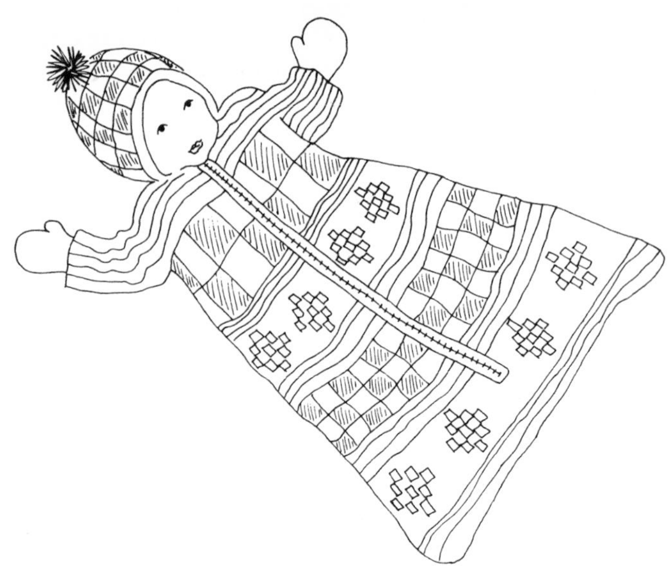

BUNTING IN GEOMETRIC DESIGN

This bunting is made of bright-colored knitting worsted to keep a little one warm and cozy. It is worked in single and double crochet in what you might call crochet's equivalent of Fair Isle knitting where 2 or more colors are used for the design. If you are not familiar with this technique, make a little practice swatch first. You may add a lining to the bunting if you wish for added warmth and softness.

SHOWN IN COLOR

SIZE: Birth to 6 months. Bunting measures 25″ from shoulder to lower edge. Width across back from underarm to underarm is 15″.
MATERIALS: Coats and Clark's Red Heart knitting worsted, 2 (4-oz.) skeins each lilac no. 586 and medium gold no. 601, 1

skein each tangerine no. 253, burnt orange no. 255 and deep turquoise no. 514; aluminum crochet hook size E **or the size that will give you the correct gauge;** 20″ neckline zipper; 1¾ yds. 36″-wide lining material (flannel, calico printed cotton or quilted fabric).

GAUGE: 4 sc = 1″; 4 rows sc = 1″.

BACK: Starting at lower edge with lilac, ch 73.

1st row (right side): Sc in 2nd ch from hk and each ch across (72 sc). Ch 1, turn.

2nd row: Sc in each sc across to within last sc. Always change colors as follows: Insert hk in next sc, draw up lp (2 lps on hk), draw lp of new color through the 2 lps on hk; break off old color, leaving 4″ end for weaving through work. Ch 1, turn.

3rd row: With turquoise, sc in each sc across. Ch 1, turn.

Working in sc patt as established, follow chart from 4th row through 13th row. (**Note:** Chart shows right front of bunting. For back, work the color indicated for the row you are on, completely across row.)

14th (dec) row: With gold, draw up a lp in each of first 2 sc (3 lps on hk), y o, draw yarn through all 3 lps on hk (1 st dec), sc across to within last 2 sc, draw up a lp in each of next 2 sc, draw yarn through all 3 lps on hk (1 st dec—70 sts). Ch 2, turn.

15th row (right side): Working dc instead of sc and following chart from A to B, sk first sc (ch 2 for turning counts as first dc), work 1 dc in each of next 12 sc, with lilac draw lp through last 2 lps of last gold dc (hold color not in use on wrong side of work and crochet so that unused color is caught along top edge of previous row and concealed in every 3rd st in solid areas between motifs); work lilac dc in each of next 2 sc, work gold dc in each of next 12 sc, work lilac dc in each of next 2 sc, work medium gold dc in each of next 6 sc. Complete row by working from B to A. Ch 2, turn.

Following chart for design, work next 4 rows in dc. Ch 1, turn.

Working in sc patt, work 2 rows of medium gold, decreasing 1 st at beg and end of first row (68 sc). Continuing in sc patt, work 2 rows lilac, 1 row deep turquoise, 3 rows burnt orange, 1 row tangerine and 2 rows deep turquoise, decreasing 1 st at beg and end of last row (66 sc). Ch 2, turn.

Starting with 31st row of chart, follow chart in established manner through 68th row, decreasing at beg and end of row as before, where indicated (58 sts).

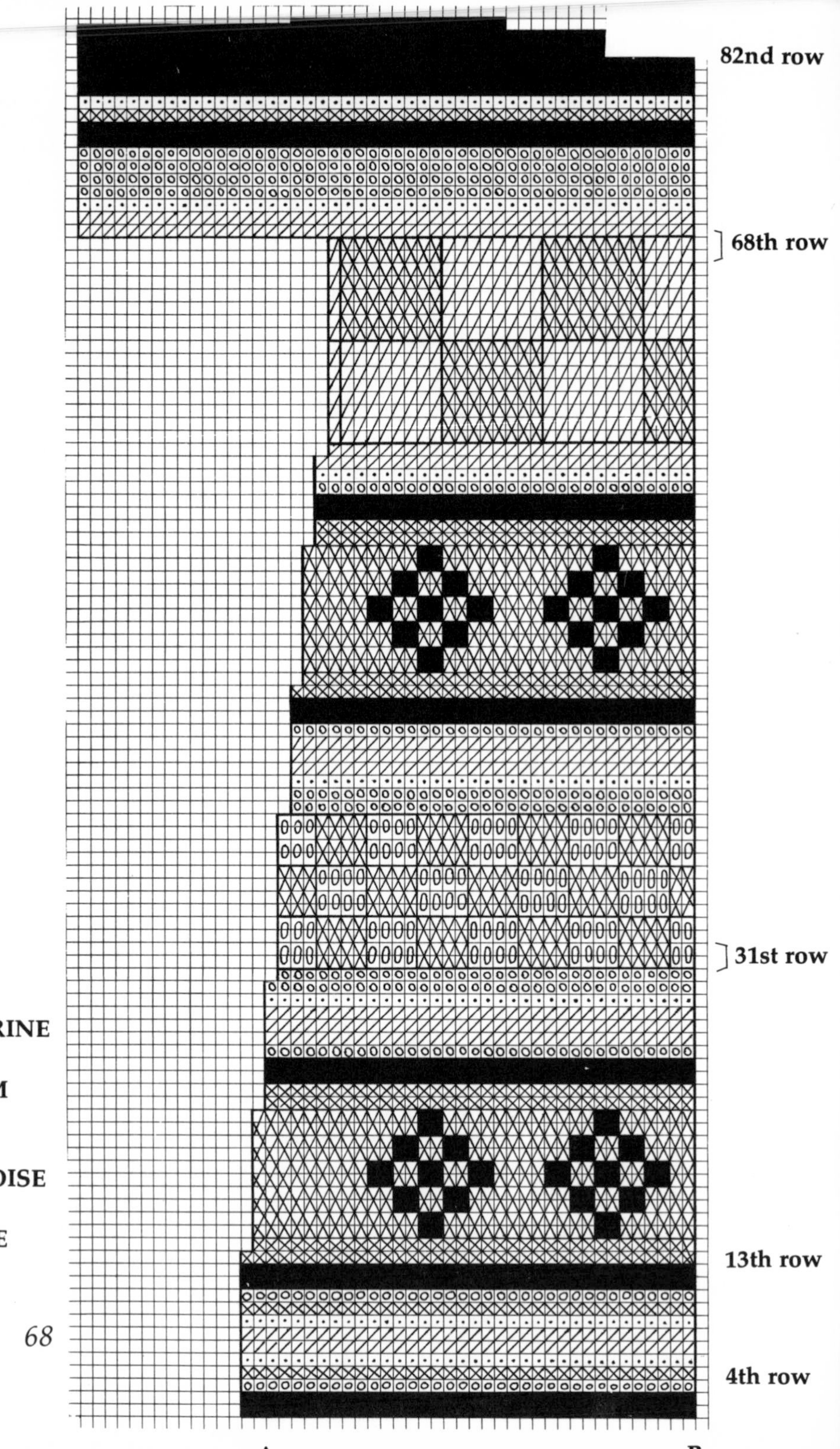

COLOR KEY

SC	DC	
■	■	LILAC
⊡	▯	TANGERINE
⊠	⊠	MEDIUM GOLD
⊙	0	DEEP TURQUOISE
◩	⧄	BURNT ORANGE

69th row: With burnt orange, ch 21 for sleeve, sc in 2nd ch from hk and each ch across (20 sc), work in sc patt across 58 sc of back, do not break off, but ch 21 for 2nd sleeve; turn.
70th row: Sc in 2nd ch from hk and each ch across, then continue to sc across 58 sc of back and 20 sc of first sleeve (98 sc). Ch 1, turn. Follow chart through 82nd row.
Sleeve and Shoulder Shaping: Note: Chart shows front shaping only. Work back shaping as follows: Work 2 more rows lilac. Sl st across first 20 sc, sc in each of next 14 sc. Break off. Sk center 30 sc for back neck, attach yarn to next sc, sc in each of next 14 sc, sl st across remaining 20 sc. Break off.

RIGHT FRONT: Starting at lower edge with lilac, ch 37.
1st row (right side): Sc in 2nd ch from hk and each ch across (36 sc). Work in patt as for back until 13 rows have been completed.
14th row (dec row): Dec 1 sc (side edge), sc in each sc across (35 sc).

Continue to work in pattern through 68th row on chart, working dec rows at side edge as indicated.
69th row: With burnt orange, sc across, do not break off, but ch 21 for sleeve; turn.
70th row: Sc in 2nd ch from hk and in each ch across, then continue to sc across 29 sc of right front (49 sc).

Follow chart over these 49 sts through 82nd row, ending at front edge.
Neck, Sleeve and Shoulder Shaping: 83rd row: Sl st across first 7 sc for neck, sc in each sc to end. Ch 1, turn.
84th row: Sc in each sc to sl sts. Ch 1, turn.
85th row: Sl st across first 8 sc, sc in each of next 17 sc, sl st to end. Break off.

LEFT FRONT: Work as for right front through 68th row, reversing shapings. For sleeve, after completion of 68th row, ch 21 with burnt orange. Sc in 2nd ch from hk and in each ch across, then with right side of left front facing you, sc in each sc across (49 sc). Complete front. Break off.

HOOD: Starting at neck edge with deep turquoise, ch 54.
1st row (right side): Dc in 4th ch from hk, dc in each of next 2 ch, * with gold, dc in each of next 4 ch, with deep turquoise dc in each of next 4 ch. Rep from * 5 times more (52 dc). Ch 2, turn.

HOOD

Top seam

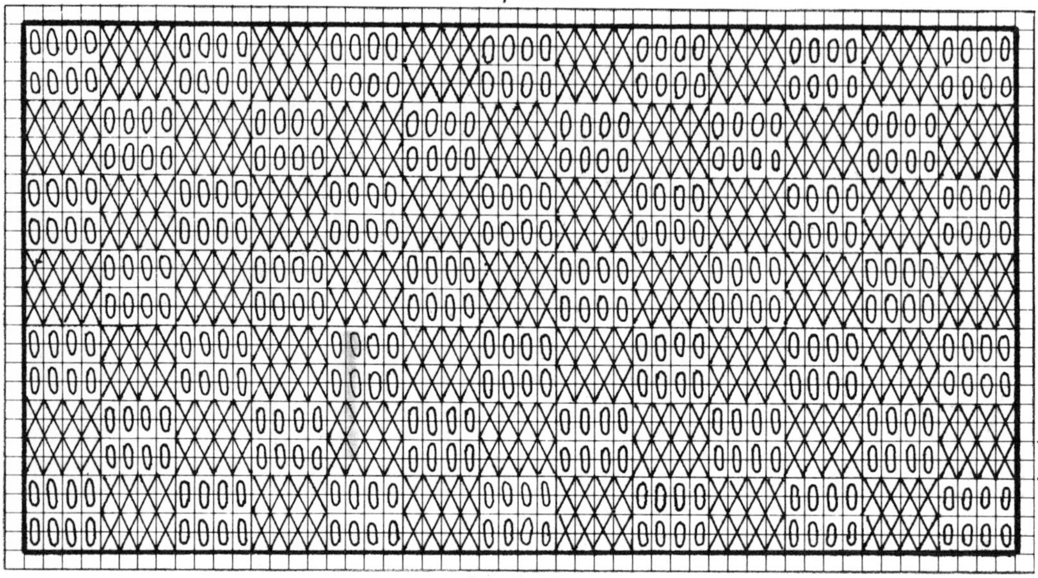

Face edge

Neck edge

2nd row: With deep turquoise sk first dc, dc in each of next 3 dc, * with gold dc in each of next 4 dc, with turquoise dc in each of next 4 dc. Repeat from * 5 times more. With gold ch 2, turn.

Starting with 3rd row of hood chart, complete hood.

FINISHING: See Royal Blue Bunting, page 109.

LINING PATTERN: See general directions for Royal Blue Bunting.

TO ASSEMBLE BUNTING: Work same as for Royal Blue Bunting. Fold hood in half crosswise and sew top seam. Sew hood to neck edge of bunting, leaving 7 sc at each front free.

TRIM: With lilac, work same as for Royal Blue Bunting. Work 1 row of sc evenly around sleeve edges.

TO INSERT LINING: See general directions for Royal Blue Bunting.

POMPOM: See page 25. Use all the colors in the bunting for a multicolored pompom. Tie pompom to hood.

AFGHAN COAT WITH CROSS-STITCH EMBROIDERY

Two faraway and exotic places have contributed their designs and techniques to this coat. It is sure to appeal to any child's imagination.

The coat is worked in the afghan stitch which originated, as the name indicates, in Afghanistan, and is decorated with cross-stitch designs inspired by the naive Peruvian folk-art motifs, which were usually embroidered in bright-colored yarns.

SHOWN IN COLOR

The afghan stitch is simple to learn, and since the stitches form an almost perfect square, they are an ideal background for cross-stitch embroidery.

As you will see, the wrong side of the afghan stitch has a nice, woven-like texture. So, you could also use it wrong side out, with just the looped fringe as decoration. Or, you may want to do the coat itself in a color and work the fringe and embroidery in a contrasting color.

The afghan stitch with cross-stitch embroidery can be applied to many designs; it would make a warm blanket or carriage cover, a bunting, hat or booties.

SIZE: 8–12 months. Coat measures 14½″ from shoulder to lower edge, 12″ across back at underarms. Side seam measures 10″, sleeve length, 6″.
MATERIALS: Bear Brand Win-Knit (100 percent orlon acrylic knitting worsted weight yarn), 3 (4-oz.) skeins winter-white no. 430; 2 oz. red synthetic knitting worsted weight yarn for embroidery; 14″-long afghan hook, size G **or the size that will give you the correct gauge;** aluminum crochet hook size G; 1 tapestry needle.
GAUGE: 5 sts = 1″; 4 rows = 1″.
Note: If you are not familiar with the afghan stitch, see page 30 for detailed instructions on how to work it. Make a little swatch with a couple of decreases and the slip-stitch row for practice.

BACK: Starting at lower edge, ch 70 to measure about 14″. Work 6 rows even in afghan st.
7th (dec) row: Insert hk under next 2 vertical bars (remember the lp which remains on hk at end of row always counts as the first st of the next row), and draw up 1 lp, work in patt across to within last 3 vertical bars from end, insert hk under next 2 vertical bars and draw up 1 lp, work last st as usual. Complete row in patt (1 st dec at beg and end of row—68 sts).

Continue in pattern and repeat dec row every 7th row 4 times more (you will notice that the decs become visible on the 6th row, so be careful counting your rows). Work even on 60 sts until 40 rows in all have been completed.

Mark beg and end of last row for beg of armholes. Then work even until 57 rows have been completed in all.
To Shape Shoulders and Back Neck: Work 1 row even across 19 sts only for right shoulder.
Sl st row: Make a sl st in each of next 18 vertical bars of right shoulder to keep edge from curling. Break off.
Back Neck: Attach yarn with sl st to right-hand neck corner and sl st in each of next 22 vertical bars for neck edge. Do not break off, but pull up a lp in each of next 18 vertical bars (19 lps on hk) for left shoulder, and complete row. Work sl st row as for right shoulder. Break off.

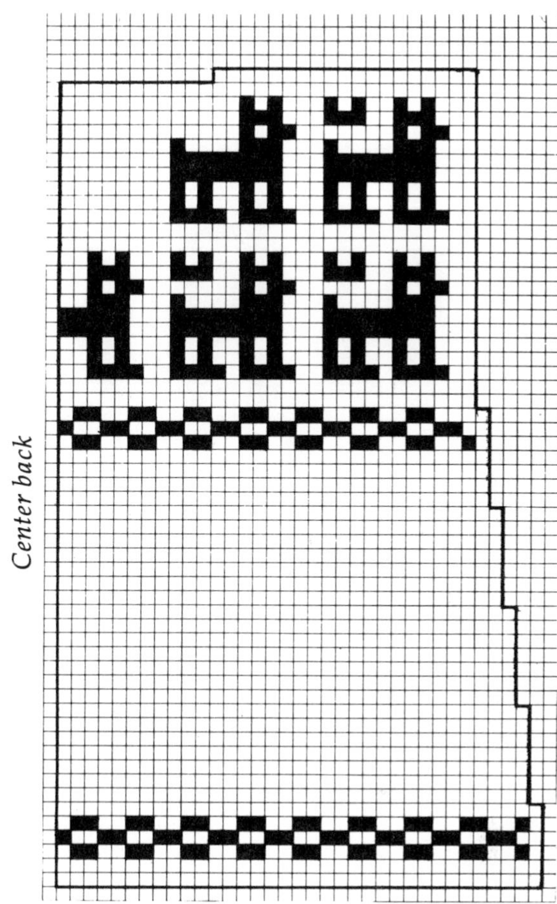

Edging: Attach white at right front neck edge, with right side of work facing you, working sts evenly spaced, and keeping edges smooth and flat, work 1 row sc along neck edge, left front and lower edge. Mark right front for 3 buttonholes, the first one at neck edge, the other two 2½″ apart. Work along right front to first pin (ch 3, sk ½″ of edge, sc to next pin) twice, ch 3, join with sl st to first sc. Break off.

Buttons: Make 3: With red, ch 4. Join with sl st to form ring.

1st rnd: Ch 1, work 10 sc in ring.

2nd rnd: (Sc in next sc, sk next sc) 5 times. Break off and leave a 7″ end. Thread this end in tapestry needle and sew up hole at top of button with a couple of small sts. Then pull thread to other side of button. Sew buttons in place.

Knitted Clothes

Knitting is a soothing pastime. It is interesting to know that until the not-too-distant past, knitting was considered a very masculine skill. Think of the ancient traders who, on top of their camels, knitted their way through Far Eastern deserts. These men ultimately brought knitting to our shores—via Egypt, Italy and France. The Middle Ages saw knitting reach its peak of perfection. Young men wanting to become master knitters spent long years learning the trade and only after passing difficult examinations would they be accepted into the knitters' guilds.

In the south of France, shepherds, standing on stilts in marshy fields, still carry on this manly craft. It is a lovely sight to see them standing there, very still, with yarn in a shoulder pouch, holding needles and stilts clutched under their arms, watching the sheep and knitting at the same time.

Around the turn of the century, knitting became very much a grandmotherly pastime. It isn't the boring knitting of yesteryear. Old techniques, such as Fair Isle, argyle and lace knitting have made a strong comeback. And today it's the creative woman who combines the best of all periods.

Here is a collection of knitted clothes for babies, inspired by the techniques and traditions of many lands. There is a fragile long christening dress and bonnet in a delicate snowdrop pattern, a soft fluffy mohair shawl, zip-up buntings, a Shetland lace kimono and booties, a Norwegian sleeper, hats, mittens, slippers and much more.

TECHNIQUES

Before you start a project, be sure to check your gauge. That is very important in obtaining the correct size. See page 17.

Yarn and knitting-needle size are specified for each project. If you are a beginning knitter, see page 20 for an explanation of the terms and abbreviations to help you decipher the instructions.

After completing your project, see page 22 on how to finish your work—that is washing, blocking and sewing it together.

Here is more specific information on knitting.

GARTER STITCH PATTERN: Knit every row.

STOCKINETTE STITCH: Knit 1 row, purl 1 row.

REVERSE STOCKINETTE STITCH: This means that the purl side is used as the right side of the work.

RIBBING: A combination of knit and purl stitches alternating across a row. The most used combination is k l, p 1 or k 2, p 2. If the row ends with a purl stitch, begin the next row with a knit stitch and vice versa. It is most often used for cuffs, neck edges and waistbands, because of its elasticity. But, of course you could work an entire garment in ribbing.

TO INCREASE: Knit or purl in front of stitch, leave it on the needle and then knit or purl in back of this same stitch.

TO DECREASE: Knit or purl 2 stitches together.

HOW TO COUNT BOUND-OFF STITCHES: When directions say bind off 5 stitches at beginning of a row, knit the first 2 stitches loosely and in pattern. Pick up first stitch with needle and pull it over the second. You have now bound off 1 stitch. So, you really have to knit 6 stitches to bind off 5, but the 6th stitch, already knitted, is on the right-hand needle.

JOINING A NEW STRAND OF YARN: Always attach a new skein of yarn at the beginning of a row. With new yarn, make a slipknot around old yarn and slide knot close to work.

If you run out of yarn in the middle of a row, and you are a terrible perfectionist, pull out the row to the beginning, because you'll always notice the joining. However, if you are a little less compulsive, leave a 4″ end of old yarn, work next stitch with new yarn, leaving a 4″ end also. Work a couple of rows, and tie ends together without pulling your work.

PICOT HEM: This is a lovely and very elastic way of finishing a hem and perfect for baby clothes.

Cast on the required number of stitches, work to the desired depth of hemfacing in stockinette stitch. Ending on wrong side of work, work an eyelet row as follows: K 1, * y o, k 2 tog. Repeat from * across the row. This row is the folding line for hem. Be careful to count your stitches to make sure you have the same number you started with. With all those yarn overs, it is easy to end up with more stitches. Starting with a purl row, continue in stockinette stitch.

WEAVING SEAMS TOGETHER: This is the most continuous

and invisible way of seaming 2 pieces of knitting together (for example, the toe of a sock, or a shoulder seam).

WEAVING OR KITCHENER STITCH: Use 2 knitting needles and a tapestry needle. Break off the working strand (that is, the strand attached to the knitting itself), leaving a 15″ end. Thread tapestry needle with this end. Make sure you have an equal number of stitches on both needles.

Hold knitting needles even and parallel, with yarn coming from the right-hand end of back needle. * Draw tapestry needle knit-wise through first stitch of front needle and slip stitch off needle; draw tapestry needle purl-wise through 2nd stitch, and leave stitch on needle. Draw tapestry needle purl-wise through first stitch on back needle, slip this stitch off needle, draw tapestry needle knit-wise through 2nd stitch of back needle, leaving stitch on needle. Repeat from * across until all stitches are woven together. Draw end through last loop and fasten off.

FAIR ISLE KNITTING: Geographical Note: Fair Isle is one of the many Shetland Islands off the north coast of Scotland, where the most intricately patterned sweaters are knitted of fine homespun and natural-dyed yarns.

Fair Isle Knitting is a technique of knitting using the stockinette stitch in a design where 2 or more colors are used across the row and the colors change every few stitches. The yarn not being used is carried on the wrong side of the work throughout. The color yarn used most is held in the right hand as usual (unless, of course, you're left-handed). Other colors are held in the left hand and worked with the left hand where required.

If the yarn not being used is carried more than 3 stitches, catch it in the knitting. This will avoid long loops on the back.

Lock the carried yarn in place as follows:

* Insert the right needle as usual, but before picking up yarn to work this stitch, slip right-hand needle under the carried yarn(s), work stitch in regular manner, slipping off carried yars) as stitch is completed. Work next 2 stitches as usual.

Repeat from * across. Don't pull yarn too tightly or your work will pucker, or too loosely, as loops will droop in the back.

BOBBIN KNITTING: A bobbin of yarn is attached when a

motif has to be worked which is not repeated across the row, as in Fair Isle knitting.

To avoid holes in your work when changing colors, work as follows:

On knit rows: Mark right side of work. Make sure bobbins are hanging on the wrong side.

Drop old color, pick up new color and bring it up from underneath the dropped color, work next stitch. Old color is caught through loop of new color on wrong side.

On purl rows: Twist yarns by bringing old color to the left side and new color to the right side. Do not carry any yarn across the back. Break off bobbin when design is completed, leaving an end long enough to weave in.

To make your own bobbins, instead of using the plastic ones, see page 21.

STRIPED TANK TOP AND SOAKERS

This two-piece suit is practical year round. It can be worn on the beach in summer, and if your baby hasn't outgrown it yet, put a pair of tights and a sweater under it to make it last when the days get cooler. Aqua top is worked in stockinette stitch with garter-stitch stripes and yoke.

Soakers, in bright green reverse stockinette stitch with a garter stitch edging, are worked in one triangular piece.

SHOWN IN COLOR

SIZE: 6–12 months. Tank top measures 20″ around chest, and 9″ from shoulder to lower edge. Soakers will stretch to fit a 20″ waist. Length from top of waistband to crotch is 8½″.
MATERIALS: Sport yarn (100 percent wool and machine washable); for tank top: 1 (2-oz.) skein light aqua, small amounts of bright green and dark turquoise; for soakers: 1 skein bright green; knitting needles, 1 pair no. 2 **or the size that will give you the correct gauge;** 1 aluminum crochet hook size B for trim only.
GAUGE: 7 sts = 1″; 10 rows = 1″.

TANK TOP

FRONT: Starting at lower edge with light aqua, cast on 74 sts. Work 5 rows in garter st (k every row). Then starting with a k row, work 6 rows in stockinette st. Break off light aqua; attach bright green. With bright green work 6 rows in garter st AND AT THE SAME TIME when piece measures 1″ from beg, dec 1 st at beg and end of next row, then every inch 4 times more (64 sts).

Break off bright green; attach light aqua. Starting with a k row and light aqua, work 4 rows in stockinette st. Break off light aqua; attach dark turquoise. With dark turquoise work 2 rows in garter st. Break off dark turquoise; attach light aqua. Starting with a k row and light aqua, work 4 rows in stockinette st. Continue in stripe patt as established (6 rows bright green in garter st, 4 rows light aqua in stockinette st, 2 rows dark turquoise in garter st and 4 rows light aqua in stockinette st) until 3 bright green stripes have been completed in all. Break off bright green; attach light aqua. Starting with a k row and light aqua, work 6 rows in stockinette st. Change to garter st and work even on 64 sts until piece measures 5½″ from beg, ending on wrong side.

To Shape Armholes: Continue in garter st. Bind off 2 sts at beg of next 2 rows. Dec 1 st at beg and end of row every other row twice. Work even on 56 sts until armholes measure 1½″, ending on wrong side.

To Shape Neck: K across 18 sts. Place remaining 38 sts on a holder. Working on 18 sts on needle, dec 1 st at neck edge every other row 4 times. Work even on 14 sts until armhole measures 3½″, ending at armhole edge.

To Shape Shoulder: Bind off 7 sts at armhole edge on next row. Work 1 row even. Bind off remaining 7 sts at beg of next row. Break off.

Sl sts from holder onto left-hand needle. Attach yarn and bind off 20 sts for center front neck opening. Work remaining 18 sts as for other side, reversing shaping.

BACK: Work same as front.

FINISHING: Sew shoulder and side seams, matching stripes. With light aqua crochet 1 rnd of sc evenly around neck opening and armholes.

SOAKERS

Note: They are worked in one triangular piece.

Starting at waistband with bright green, cast on 130 sts. Work 5 rows in ribbing of k 1, p 1.

6th row (eyelet row): K 1, * y o, k 2 tog, p 1, k 1. Rep from * across, ending with p 1. Continue in ribbing as established until waistband measures 1½″ from beg.

Establish patt as follows: (**Note:** Sl first st of each row as if to knit for a nice garter st selvage.)

1st (dec) row (right side): Sl 1, k 3, sl 1, k 1, psso, p across to last 6 sts, k 2 tog, k 4.
2nd row: Sl 1, k 3, p 1, k across to last 5 sts, p 1, k 4.

Rep these 2 rows until 10 sts remain, ending on wrong side.
To Shape Tip: 1st row: Sl 1, k 3, sl 1, k 1, psso, k 4 (9 sts).
2nd and 4th rows: Sl 1, k across.
3rd row: Sl 1, k 2, k 3 tog (7 sts).

Rep 3rd and 4th rows twice more, k 1 st less before and after dec (3 sts). K 3 tog. Break off.

FINISHING: Sew ends of waistband together. Turn tip up to bottom of waistband seam and sew edges together for about 3″. With a double strand of dark turquoise, crochet a chain 30″ long. Run chain through eyelet row. Tie in front.

HAT, MITTENS AND BOOTIES SET

To brighten up any winter day, hat, mittens and booties in bright-colored stripes are worked in simple garter stitch, using acrylic knitting worsted weight yarn. They will look equally nice in a solid color, to match an outfit you may already have.

SHOWN IN COLOR

SIZE: Infant. Hat measures 5½″ from top of crown to face edge and will stretch to measure 17″ around. Mittens are 5″ from tip of mitten to cuff edge. Booties measure 4″ from heel to toe and 4½″ from heel to top edge.
MATERIALS: Synthetic knitting worsted weight yarn, 2 oz. each dark rose, red, orange and pink; knitting needles, 1 pair no. 5, **or the size that will give you the correct gauge.**
GAUGE: In garter st, 5 sts and 9 rows = 1″.

BOOTIES

Starting at sole edge with dark rose, cast on 40 sts. Work 4 rows even in garter st (first row is wrong side of work). Break off dark rose. Then continuing in garter st, work 4 rows each red, orange, pink and 2 rows dark rose.

Bind off 8 sts at beg of next 2 rows (24 sts). Break off dark rose, attach red. Work 1 row even.
Next (eyelet) row: K 1, * y o, k 2 tog. Rep from * across, ending with k 1.

K 2 rows even. Break off red. Continuing in garter st and stripe pattern as established, work even until piece measures 5½″ from beg, ending with a dark rose stripe. Bind off loosely.
FINISHING: Weave in ends on wrong side. Sew front, toe and sole seams, matching stripes.
Cord: Make 2. Cut 2 strands red each 1 yd. long. Hold together and knot each end. Twist these strands tightly in one direc-

tion. Hold center of cord and bring knotted ends together. Let cord twist around itself. Make a knot 1/2″ from each end. Trim strands to form a small tassel. Weave cord through eyelet row.

MITTENS

Starting at edge of cuff, with dark rose, cast on 22 sts. Work 10 rows in garter st. Break off dark rose. With red k 1 row.

Next (eyelet) row: K 1, * y o, k 2 tog. Rep from * across, ending with k 1.

Continuing in garter st, work 2 rows red, then 4 rows each orange, pink, dark rose, red, orange and pink.

To Shape Tip: With dark rose, k 2 rows.

3rd row: * k 1, k 2 tog. Rep from * across, ending with k 1 (15 sts).

4th and 6th rows: K across.

5th row: * K 2 tog, k 1, repeat from * across.

7th row: K 2 tog across.

Break off, leaving a 6″ end. Thread end in a tapestry needle and draw through last 5 sts on needle. Pull up tight and fasten off. Sew side seam, being careful to match stripes.

Make a cord as for booties and weave through eyelet row.

Make another red cord 36″ long as before, sew a mitten to each end, put the cord through the sleeves of coat or jacket. This will prevent mittens from getting lost.

HAT

Starting at lower edge with dark rose, cast on 64 sts, and work 8 rows even in garter st. Then continue in patt and work 4 rows each red, orange, pink, dark rose, red, orange and pink.

To Shape Crown: Continuing with dark rose only, k 1 row.

2nd Row: * K 6, k 2 tog. Rep from * across.

3rd and all uneven rows: K across.

4th row: * K 5, k 2 tog. Rep from * across.

6th row: * K 4, k 2 tog. Rep from * across.

8th row: * K 3, k 2 tog. Rep from * across.

10th row: * K 2, k 2 tog. Rep from * across.

Last row: K 2 tog across (12 sts).

Break off, leaving a 12″ length of yarn. Thread end in a tapestry needle and draw through 12 sts on needle. Pull up tight and fasten off. Sew back seam, matching stripes.

Make a cord as for booties. Tie in a bow and sew to top of crown.

A WARM WOOLEN JACKET AND BOOTIES

This woolly set is made to go out on a balmy fall day. The autumnal color combination of rose and brick heather gives a tweedy effect. Complete with garter-stitch details and frog loops that close over a double row of silver buttons. There are booties to match.

SHOWN IN COLOR

SIZE: Infant. Jacket measures 10″ across at underarms, and 9½″ from shoulder to lower edge. Sleeve length is 4″. Booties measure 4″ from heel to toe and 4½″ from heel to top of cuff.
MATERIALS: Brunswick Tyrol knitting worsted (100 percent virgin wool), 2 (2-oz.) skeins rose heather no. 7872; Brunswick Fairhaven fingering yarn, 4 (1-oz.) skeins brick heather no. 1674; knitting needles, 1 pair no. 6, **or the size that will give you the correct gauge;** 6 silver buttons ⅝″ in diameter; steel crochet hook, size 0.
GAUGE: 4 sts and 5 rows = 1″.
Note: When directions say Tweed, use 1 strand each of knitting worsted and fingering yarn held together. When directions say Brick, use 3 strands of fingering yarn held together, unless specified otherwise.

JACKET

BACK: Starting at lower edge with Tweed, cast on 40 sts. Starting with a p row, work even in stockinette st until piece measures 6¼″ from beg, or desired length to underarm, ending on wrong side. Break off Tweed; attach Brick.
To Shape Armholes: From now on work in garter st with Brick. Bind off 2 sts at beg of next 2 rows. Work even on 36 sts until armholes measure 3″.
To Shape Neck: K across 12 sts. Bind off next 12 sts for back

neck, k remaining 12 sts. Work even on these last 12 sts until armhole measures 3¼″, ending at armhole edge.

To Shape Shoulder: Bind off 6 sts at beg of next row. K 1 row even. Bind off remaining 6 sts. Attach yarn at opposite neck edge and work other side to correspond, reversing shaping.

LEFT FRONT: Note: To work front border, wind a Brick bobbin. When changing colors, twist yarns by bringing new color under yarn you have been working with to avoid holes in your work.

Starting at lower edge with Tweed, cast on 20 sts, attach a separate bobbin of Brick and cast on 4 sts for front border.

1st row (wrong side): With Brick, k 4, with Tweed, p 20. Mark end of row for side edge.

2nd row: With Tweed, k 20, with Brick, k 4.

Repeating 1st and 2nd rows for patt, keeping 4 sts in garter st for front border, work even until piece measures same as back to underarms, ending on wrong side at side edge. Break off Tweed; attach Brick.

To Shape Armhole: From now on work in garter st, with Brick. Bind off 2 sts at beg of next row, k across. Work even on 22 sts until armhole measures 2½″, ending at front edge.

To Shape Neck: Bind off 10 sts at beg of next row, k across. Work even on 12 sts until armhole measures same as armhole on back, ending at armhole edge.

To Shape Shoulder: Bind off 6 sts at beg of next row, k across. Work 1 row even. Bind off remaining 6 sts.

RIGHT FRONT: Starting at lower edge with Brick bobbin, cast on 4 sts, attach Tweed and cast on 20 sts.

1st row (wrong side): With Tweed, p 20, with Brick, k 4.

2nd row: With Brick, k 4, with Tweed k across. Mark end of this row for side edge.

Repeating 1st and 2nd rows for patt, work even until piece measures 6¼″ from beg, ending at front edge.

Next row: With Brick, k 4. Break off Tweed, leaving a 3″ end, and with Brick continue to k across.

To Shape Armhole: From now on work in garter st with Brick. Bind off 2 sts at beg of next row, k across.

Complete front to correspond to left front, reversing all shapings.

SLEEVES: Starting at cuff with Brick, cast on 26 sts. Work 7 rows even in garter st. Break off Brick; attach Tweed. Starting with a k row, work even in stockinette st until sleeve measures

4″ from beg, or desired length to underarm. Bind off.

FINISHING: With overhand stitch (see page 25) sew shoulder seams. Sew sleeves in place. Sew underarm and side seams. Sew 3 buttons inside each front border, the first one at neck edge, the next 2 each 2″ below each other.

Button Loops: Make 3. With Tweed, ch 20, being careful not to twist chain, join with sl st to first ch to form a lp. Break off. Twist lp to form a figure 8. Tack at center of twist. Sew to center of right front band at neck, the other 2 to correspond with buttons. Slip lps over buttons.

Edging: With Brick, work 1 row of reverse sc evenly around wrist edges, neck, front and lower edges. See page 32 for reverse sc.

BOOTIES

Starting at sole with Tweed, cast on 32 sts. Starting with a p row, work in stockinette st, until piece measures 2″ from beg, ending on wrong side.

Bind off 6 sts at beg of next 2 rows (20 sts).

Next row (eyelet row): K 1, * y o, k 2 tog. Repeat from * across, ending with k 1.

Starting with a p row, work in stockinette st until piece measures 1″ from eyelet row, ending on wrong side.

Break off Tweed; attach Brick. In garter st work 1″ even, ending on wrong side. Bind off. Make 2nd bootie in same manner.

FINISHING: Sew front, toe and sole seams.

Ties (make 2): With Brick make a chain 13″ long. Weave through eyelet row. Knot each end of tie. Tie in front.

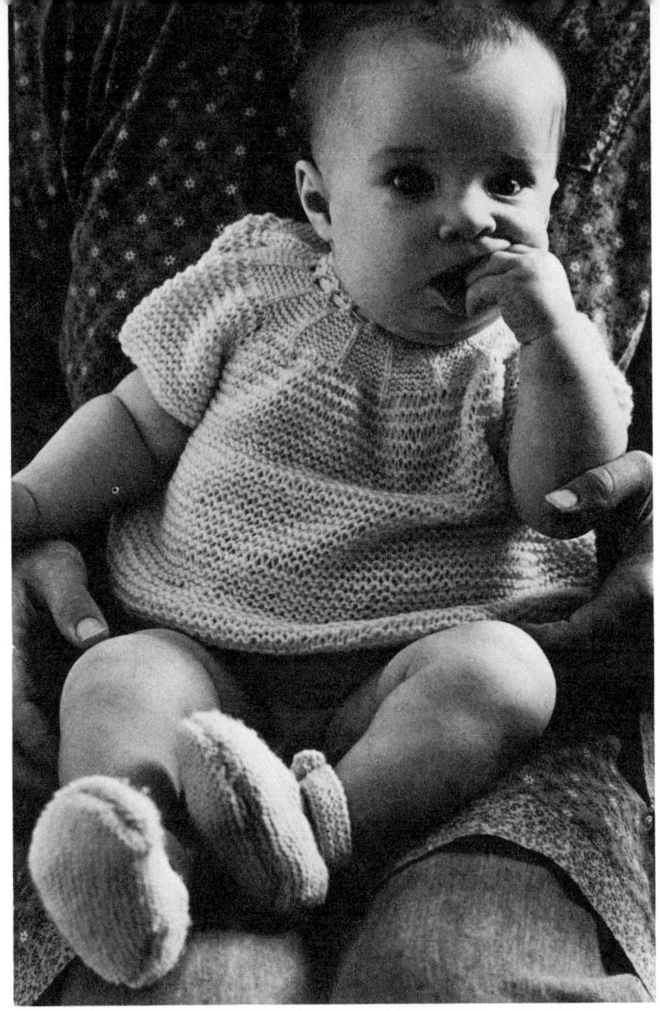

GARTER DROP-STITCH SMOCK AND SLIPPERS

Any beginner can knit this little set in the basic garter stitch. The garter drop-stitch smock works up double quickly. "Dropping the yarn over" is like doing 2 rows at a time and this gives the work a nice open effect. The slippers are in plain garter stitch.

SIZE: 3 months. Smock measures 10″ across front from underarm to underarm. Length is 9½″ from shoulder to lower edge.

Sleeve length is 2". Sole of slippers measures 4" from heel to toe.

MATERIALS: Brunswick Delf-baby (100% acrylic) yarn, 3 (1-oz.) skeins baby pink no. 1201; knitting needles, 1 pair each of no. 1 and no. 2 **or the size that will give you the correct gauge;** 1 yd. of 1/4"-wide pink ribbon; 1 aluminum crochet hook size B; 2 buttons 3/8" in diameter.

GAUGE: With no. 1 needles:

Garter drop st: 5 sts and 8 rows = 1".

Garter st: 7 sts and 15 rows = 1".

SMOCK

FRONT: Starting at lower edge with no. 2 needles, cast on 65 sts. Work 5 rows in garter st (k every row) for border. Establish pattern as follows: Change to no. 1 needles.

1st row (right side): K 1, * y o, k 1. Rep from * across.

2nd row: K across, dropping each y o.

Repeating these 2 rows for patt, work even until piece measures 6" from beg, ending with a 2nd patt row.

To Shape Armholes: Bind off 2 sts at beg of next 2 rows. Dec 1 st at beg and end of every other row 6 times (49 sts), ending with a 2nd patt row. Place these stitches on a holder.

RIGHT BACK: Starting at lower edge with no. 2 needles, cast on 40 sts. Work 5 rows in garter st, marking end of last row for side edge. Change to no. 1 needles. Work even in patt as before until piece measures same as front to underarm, ending with a 2nd patt row at side edge.

To Shape Armhole: Bind off 2 sts at beg (armhole edge) of next row. Dec 1 st at armhole edge every other row 6 times (32 sts). Work 1 row even, ending with a 2nd patt row. Place these sts on a holder.

LEFT BACK: Cast on as for right back. Work 5 rows in garter st for border. Mark beg of last row for side edge. Work same as for right back until piece measures same as front to underarm, ending with a first patt row.

To Shape Armhole: Bind off 2 sts at beg (armhole edge) of next row. Dec 1 st at armhole edge every other row 6 times (32 sts), ending with a 2nd patt row. Place these sts on a holder.

SLEEVES: Starting at lower edge with no. 1 needles, cast on 35 sts. Work 5 rows in garter st, inc 8 sts evenly spaced on last row (43 sts). Work even in patt until piece measures 1½" from beg, ending with a 2nd patt row.

To Shape Armholes: Work same as for front. Place remaining 27 sts on a holder.

YOKE: Hold a needle in left hand and, with right side of work facing you, slip pieces onto it in the following order: right back, sleeve, front, second sleeve and left back (167 sts).

1st row (right side): K across, dec 28 sts as evenly spaced as possible (139 sts).

2nd row: K 5, * p 1, k 7. Rep from * across, ending with k 5.

3rd row: K across.

Rep 2nd and 3rd rows 3 times more, then repeat 2nd row once more.

11th (dec) row: K 6, * k 2 tog, k 3, sl 1, k 1, psso, k 1.

Rep from * across, ending with k 6 (107 sts).

12th row: K 5, * p 1, k 5. Rep from * across.

13th row: K across.

Rep 12th and 13th rows once more, then rep 12th row once more.

17th (dec) row: K 3, sl 1, k 1, psso, k 1, * k 2 tog, k 1, sl 1, k 1, psso, k 1. Rep from * across to last 5 sts, k 2 tog, k 3 (73 sts).

18th row: K 4, * p 1, k 3. Rep from * across, ending with k 4.

19th row: K across.

Next (eyelet) row: K 1, * y o, k 2 tog. Rep from * across, k 4 rows even. Bind off loosely.

FINISHING: Sew side, sleeve and underarm seams. With right side of work facing you, starting at upper corner of right back, work 1 row of sc evenly along right back, lower and left back edges, working 3 sc in corners.

Thread ribbon through eyelet row. Sew ribbon to end of eyelet row at each back neck edge to keep it from tightening.

SLIPPERS

SOLE: Starting at side edge of sole, with no. 1 needles, cast on 22 sts. K 2 rows even. Continue in garter st, inc 1 st at beg of each row until there are 40 sts on needle. K 3 rows even, then dec 1 st at end of each row until 22 sts remain. The sole is completed now, but do not break off.

SIDES AND TOP:

1st row: K across, then cast on 12 sts for heel.

2nd row: K to within last 2 sts, inc 1 st in next st, k 1 (toe).

3rd row: K across.

Rep these last 2 rows until there are 43 sts on needle, ending at heel.

To Shape Heel: 1st row: K 12, turn.
2nd and all even rows: K across.
3rd row: K 9, turn.
5th row: K 6, turn.
7th row (heel edge): Bind off 23 sts, k 20 (side of slipper completed).
For Top of Toe: Working across these 20 sts, work 14 rows even. To work opposite side of slipper, k 20, cast on 23 sts.
1st row: K 6, turn.
2nd and all even rows: K across.
3rd row: K 9, turn.
5th row: K 12, turn.
7th row: K across to last 3 sts, k 2 tog, k 1.
8th row: K across.

Rep 7th and 8th rows until 34 sts remain. K 1 row even. Bind off.

STRAP: With no. 1 needle, cast on 48 sts. K 2 rows even.
3rd row: (buttonhole row): K 3, y o, k 2 tog, k across. K 2 rows even. Bind off.
FINISHING: Sew heel seam. Sew top to sole at toe and heel. Sew strap to top edge of heel. Sew buttons in place. With size B hk, sc evenly around top opening and straps.

DRESS IN VARIEGATED YARN

The skirt and sleeves of this fashionable little dress are worked in a multicolored, variegated knitting worsted. The bodice is solid green—red and blue ribbing finishes off neck edge. The dress zips up the back. Garter-stitch edges keep work from curling.

SHOWN IN COLOR

SIZE: 9–12 months. Dress measures 11″ across chest from side seam to side seam, 12″ from shoulder to lower edge; skirt length is 7″. Sleeve length is 1½″.
MATERIALS: Bucilla de Luxe knitting worsted (100 percent wool), 2 (3½-oz.) skeins confetti ombre no. 011, 2 oz. emerald green no. 93, 1 oz. each royal blue no. 20 and scarlet no. 309; knitting needles, 1 pair no. 5 **or the size that will give you the correct gauge;** 7″ neckline zipper.
GAUGE: 5 sts and 6 rows = 1″.

Note: Dress is worked in one piece without side seams. Sleeves are worked separately and sewn in.
SKIRT: Starting at lower edge with confetti, cast on 200 sts, work 3 rows in garter st for border. Then starting with a k row, work in stockinette st until skirt measures 7″ from beg, ending on wrong side, dec 89 sts as evenly spaced as possible on last row (111 sts). Break off confetti; attach emerald green.
BODICE: Starting with a k row, work 1″ even in stockinette st, ending on wrong side.
To Divide Work: Work across 28 sts, for left back, sl next 55 sts onto a holder for front, sl last 28 sts onto another holder for right back.
LEFT BACK: Working over these 28 sts only in stockinette st,

bind off 3 sts at beg of next row (armhole edge), then dec 1 st at same edge, every other row 3 times, work even on 22 sts until armhole measures 3¼", ending at back edge.

To Shape Neck: Bind off 11 sts at beg of next row, then dec 1 st at neck edge every other row 3 times, work even on 8 sts until armhole measures 4¼", ending at armhole edge.

To Shape Shoulder: Bind off 4 sts at beg of next row. Work 1 row even. Bind off remaining 4 sts.

FRONT: Slip 55 sts of front onto left-hand needle, attach emerald green and work across these 55 sts in patt. Bind off 3 sts at beg of next 2 rows, then dec 1 st at beg and end of every other row 3 times. Work even on 43 sts until armhole measures 2¼",. ending on wrong side.

To Shape Neck: Work across 14 sts, bind off 15 center sts, work across last 14 sts. Working over these 14 sts only, dec 1 st at neck edge, every other row 6 times. Work even on 8 sts until armhole measures same as back armhole, ending at armhole edge.

To Shape Shoulder: Bind off 4 sts at beg of next row. Work 1 row even. Bind off remaining 4 sts.

Attach yarn at opposite side of neck edge and complete to correspond, reversing shaping.

RIGHT BACK: Slip these 28 sts onto left-hand needle and work to correspond to left back, reversing shaping.

SLEEVES: With confetti, cast on 45 sts. Work 3 rows in garter st, then starting with a k row, work in stockinette st until sleeve measures 1½" from beg, ending on wrong side.

To Shape Cap: Dec 1 st at beg and end of every row 6 times. Work 1 row even. Bind off remaining 33 sts.

FINISHING: Sew shoulder seams. Sew sleeves in place.

Neck Ribbing: With right side of work facing you, using scarlet, pick up and k 79 sts evenly along neck edge.

1st row (wrong side): With scarlet, work in k 1, p 1 ribbing across. Break off scarlet; attach royal blue.

2nd row: With royal blue k across.

Work 2 rows even in ribbing as established. Break off royal blue; attach scarlet.

5th row: With scarlet, p across. Work 1 row in ribbing as established. Bind off in ribbing.

With right sides of backs together, starting at lower edge, sew center back seam for 5", leaving rest of back open for zipper. Sew zipper in place.

SNOWSUIT

A royal blue two-piece suit in a double-seed-stitch pattern, alternated with garter-stitch stripes, is reminiscent of the traditional patterns found on the fishermen sweaters of the English Channel Islands.

Those "jerseys," as they were called, were made of the finest yarns on the thinnest needles in intricate patterns. You could practically identify a person by just seeing the sweater which was being worn. The sweaters were genuine heirlooms which never seemed to wear out, and were handed down from father to son.

The jacket of this suit is made up of simple rectangular pieces, and zips up the back. Pants are worked in double seed stitch only.

SIZE: 9–12 months. Jacket measures 11″ across front from side seam to side seam, 9½″ from shoulder to lower edge. Sleeve

length is 6½″. Pants measure 20″ around waist, unstretched, 7½″ from waist to crotch. Inside leg seam is 8½″.
MATERIALS: Bucilla de Luxe knitting worsted (100 percent wool), 4 (4-oz.) skeins royal blue no. 20; knitting needles, 1 pair no. 5, **or the size that will give you the correct gauge;** 18″ neckline zipper.
GAUGE: 5 sts and 6 rows = 1″.

SEED-STITCH PATTERN: Worked on an even number of stitches.
1st row (wrong side): Purl across.
2nd row: K 2, p 2 across.
3rd row: P across.
4th row: P 2, k 2 across.
5th row: P across.
Rep 2nd through 5th rows twice more.
14th through 16th rows: K across.
17th row: P across.
Rep 14th through 17th rows once more.
22nd through 24th rows: K across.
Rep these 24 rows for patt (1 rep is 3¼″ long).

JACKET

FRONT: Starting at lower edge, cast on 56 sts. Work 6 rows in garter st (k every row).

Work patt twice, then rep pattern through 15th patt row.
To Shape Neck: Keeping in patt as established, work across 22 sts, place remaining 34 sts on a holder. Dec 1 st at neck edge every other row 4 times, ending with a 24th patt row. Bind off.

With right side of work facing you, sl sts from holder onto left-hand needle, attach yarn, bind off center 12 sts and work opposite side to correspond, reversing shaping. Place a marker in work at side edges 5½″ from beg to mark beg of armholes.

RIGHT BACK: Starting at lower edge, cast on 29 sts.
1st row (wrong side): K 3 for back border, work first patt row across.
2nd row: Work 2nd patt row across to within last 3 sts, k 3. Being careful to keep 3 border sts in garter st, rep patt 3 times in all. Bind off. Place marker at side edge 5½″ from beg to mark beg of armhole.

LEFT BACK: Starting at lower edge, cast on 29 sts. Establish patt as follows:
1st row: Work first patt row to within last 3 sts, k 3.
2nd row: K 3, work in patt across, complete as for right back.

SLEEVES: Starting at wrist edge, cast on 45 sts. Work 6 rows in garter st, then repeat patt twice. Bind off.

HOOD: Starting at face edge, cast on 74 sts. Work 6 rows in garter st, then repeat patt twice, then work patt once more through 6th patt row. Bind off.
FINISHING: Block pieces. Sew shoulder seams. Sew sleeves in place between markers. Sew side and sleeve seams. Fold hood in half crosswise, sew hood to neck edge, matching garter st border at center front neck edge. Do not sew back seam of hood.

Sew zipper in place at center back and hood opening.

PANTS

FRONT—LEFT LEG: Starting at lower edge, cast on 26 sts. Work 6 rows in garter st. Change to patt as follows: P 1 row. Rep 2nd through 5th rows until leg measures 9″ from beg, ending with a 2nd patt row. Place these sts on a holder.
RIGHT LEG: Work same as left leg for 9″, ending with a 2nd patt row.
Next row: P across, cast on 6 sts for crotch, with wrong side of work facing you, sl sts from holder onto left needle, and work across (58 sts), continue to work in patt as established, dec 1 st at beg and end of row every 2″ 3 times (52 sts), until piece measures 15″ from beg, ending on wrong side.
WAISTBAND: Work 4 rows in ribbing of k 1, p 1.
Eyelet row: Rib 3 sts, * k 2 tog, y o, rib 3 sts. Rep from * across, ending with rib 2. Being careful to reestablish rib patt, work 4 rows in patt. Bind off in ribbing.
FINISHING: Sew side seams, crotch and inside leg seams. Make a 34″-long twisted cord (see page 26) and weave it through eyelet row. Tie in front.

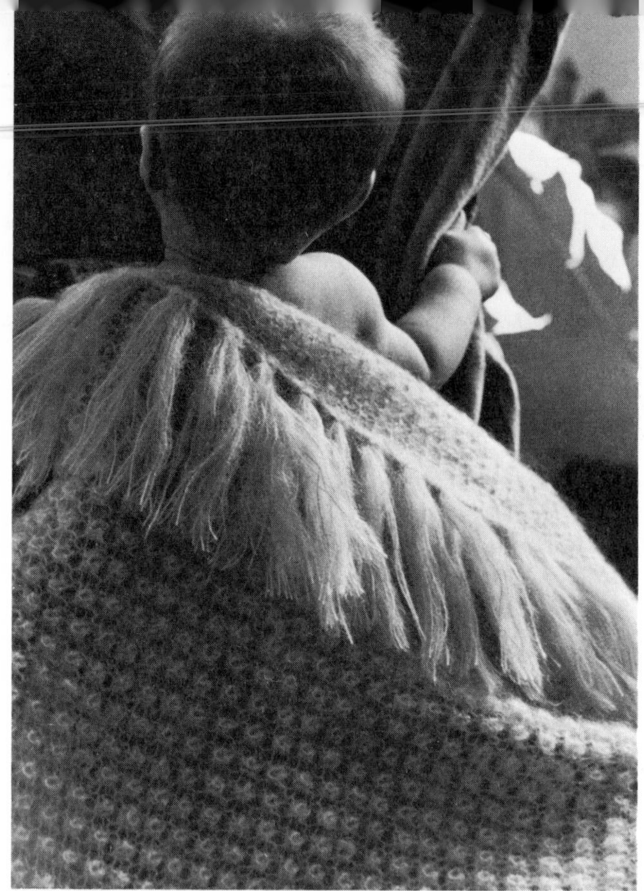

BABY SHAWL

In an airy, snowflake pattern with a garter-stitch border, this shawl is worked in a feather-light, pearly parchment-colored mohair yarn. Knits up quickly on large needles. Luxuriously fringed by tassels all around, it is ideal to wrap snugly around baby, or to drape over a carriage to keep out the drafts.

SIZE: 24″ x 37″ without fringe.
MATERIALS: Reynolds Mohair no. I (85 percent mohair, 15 percent vinyon), 10 (1-oz.) skeins Natural no. 5; knitting needles, 1 pair no. 9 **or the size that will give you the correct gauge.**
GAUGE: In garter st: 4 sts and 5 rows = 1″.
SNOWFLAKE PATTERN: Worked on a multiple of 4 sts plus 1 st.

1st row (wrong side): In same st work k 1, y o, k 1 (3 sts in 1 st); * p 3 tog, work 3 sts in next st. Rep from * across.
2nd and 4th rows: P across.
3rd row: P 3 tog, * in next st work k 1, y o, k 1 (3 sts in 1 st), p 3 tog, repeat from * across.

Rep these 4 rows for pattern.

Cast on 99 sts. Work 8 rows in garter st (k every row) for border.

Next row (wrong side): K 5, work first row of patt st across next 89 sts, then k last 5 sts.

Work 5 sts at beg and end of row in garter st for side borders and center 89 sts in patt st, until piece measures 35″ from beg, ending with a 4th patt row. Then work 9 rows in garter st for end border. Bind off loosely.

Pin out to measure 24″ x 37″. Dampen lightly (a plant mister works very well for this). Let shawl dry thoroughly before unpinning.

FRINGE: For each tassel cut twelve 10″ strands of yarn. Double strands to form a lp. With a crochet hook pull lp through a st along edge and draw loose ends through lp; pull tight. Knot tassels 1/4″ apart all around shawl.

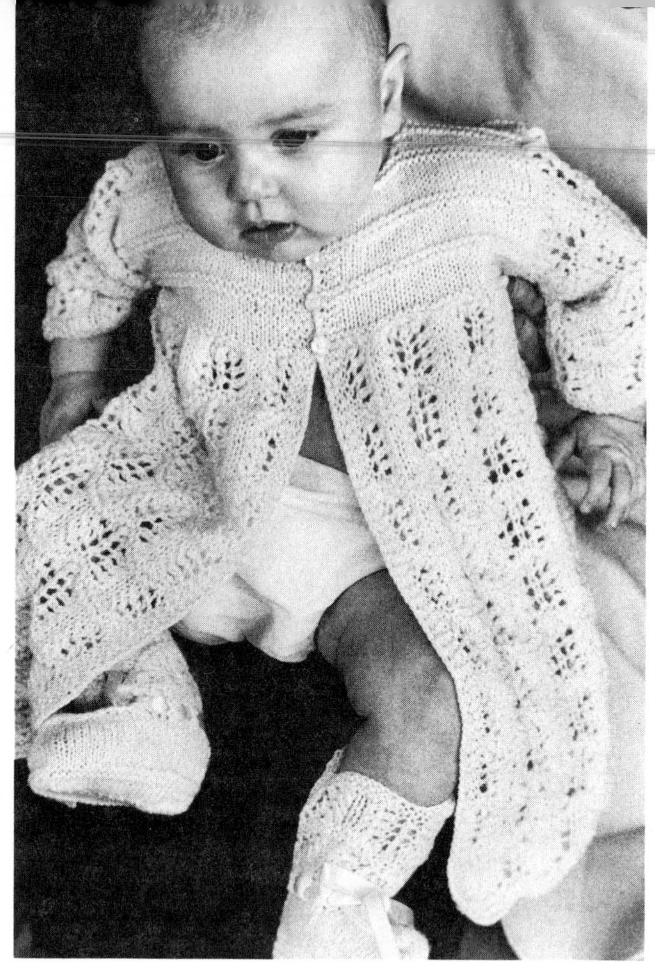

KIMONO AND BOOTIES

Dress up the little one in a long, yellow kimono in a lacy, openwork pattern, which is called "crest-of-wave," a knitted lace originating in the Shetland Islands, where the fishermen's wives tried to imitate the fine needle-made lace using their knitting needles and hair-fine woolen yarns. The yoke is worked in stockinette stitch with garter-stitch stripe details.

Cuff of booties is worked in pattern, the foot itself in stockinette stitch.

SIZE: Infant. Kimono measures 21″ around chest and 16½″

from shoulder to lower edge. Sleeves measure 6″ from wrist to underarm.

MATERIALS: Brunswick Delf-baby (100% acrylic) yarn, 4 (1-oz.) skeins baby yellow; knitting needles, 1 pair each no. 3 and no. 2 **or the size that will give you the correct gauge;** 1 steel crochet hook no. 0; 4 buttons, 3/8″ in diameter; 1 yd of 1/4″-wide satin yellow ribbon.

GAUGE: With no. 3 needles in patt st: 7 sts and 8 rows = 1″.

CREST-OF-WAVE PATTERN: Multiple of 12 plus 3.
1st through 4th rows: K across.
5th row (right side): K 2, y o, k 1, * y o, (sl 1, k 1, psso) twice, k 1, (k 2 tog) twice, (y o, k 1) 3 times. Rep from * across, to within last 3 sts, y o, k 1, y o, k 2.
6th row: P across.

Rep 5th and 6th rows 3 times more.

Rep these 12 rows for patt.

KIMONO

BACK: Starting at lower edge with no. 3 needles, cast on 87 sts. Work even in patt until piece measures 13″ from beg, ending on wrong side with a 12th patt row. K 1 row even.
To Shape Armholes: Change to no. 2 needles. Bind off 4 sts at beg of next row, k across. Bind off 4 sts at beg of following row, k across, dec 22 sts as evenly spaced as possible (57 sts). K 1 row even. Continue to work even and, starting with a k row, work 7 rows in stockinette st, then work 3 rows in garter st (k every row). Repeat these last 10 rows twice more. Starting with a k row, continue in stockinette st until armholes measure 3½″ from beg. Bind off.

RIGHT FRONT: Starting at lower edge, with no. 3 needles, cast on 52 sts. Establish patt as follows: K 4 rows, marking end of last row as front edge.
5th row (right side): K 3, y o, k 1, * y o, (sl 1, k 1, psso) twice, k 1, (k 2 tog) twice, (y o, k 1) 3 times. Rep from * across to within last 3 sts, y o, k 1, y o, k 2.
6th row: P across to last 3 sts, k 3. Rep 5th and 6th rows 3 times more. Continue to work even in patt as established until piece measures same as back to underarms, being careful to keep 3 front border sts in garter st, ending at side edge with a 12th patt row. K 1 row even.

To Shape Armhole: Change to no. 2 needles. Bind off 4 sts at beg of next row and k across.

Next row: K across, dec 16 sts as evenly spaced as possible (32 sts). K 1 row even.

Starting with a k row and keeping 3 front border sts in garter st, work 7 rows in stockinette st, then work 3 rows in garter st. Rep these last 10 rows twice more, ending at front edge.

To Shape Neck: 1st row: Bind off 12 sts at beg of next row, k across.

2nd row: P across to last 3 sts, k 3.

3rd row: K across.

Repeat 2nd row once more. Bind off.

LEFT FRONT: Cast on as for right front. Establish pattern as follows: K 4 rows, marking beg of last row as front edge.

5th row (right side): K 2, y o, k 1, * y o (sl 1, k 1, psso) twice, k 1, (k 2 tog) twice, (y o, k 1) 3 times. Rep from * across to within last 4 sts, y o, k 1, y o, k 3.

6th row: K 3, p across.

Complete as for right front, reversing all shaping.

SLEEVES: Starting at lower edge with no. 3 needles, cast on 51 sts. Work in pattern as for back until piece measures 6″ from beg, ending with a 12th patt row. Bind off.

FINISHING: Sew shoulder seams. Sew sleeves in place. Sew underarm and side seams, being careful to match garter st ribs. Sew buttons on right front yoke edge, first one at neck edge, the other 3 at each garter-st stripe on yoke.

Edging: Attach yarn with sl st to lower edge of right front, sc evenly along front edge and around neck edge, continuing along left front edge, * ch 4, sk 2 garter st ribs, sc along edge to next 2 ribs. Rep from * 3 times more, sc evenly along to lower edge. Break off.

BOOTIES

CUFF: Starting at top edge with no. 3 needles, cast on 39 sts. Work even in patt as for back until piece measures 3″ from beg, ending with a 12th patt row.

Next row: K across, dec 4 sts evenly spaced (35 sts). P 1 row. Change to no. 2 needles. P 1 row.

Eyelet row: P 1, * y o, p 2 tog. Repeat from * across. P 1 row.

INSTEP:
1st row: P 23, turn.
2nd row: K 11, turn. Starting with a p row, work 14 rows in stockinette st. Then dec 1 st at beg and end of every other row twice (7 sts). Place 7 sts on a holder. Break off.
FOOT:
1st row: With right side of work facing you, attach yarn at beg of right-hand side of instep. Pick up and k 14 sts along same side of instep, k 7 sts from holder, pick up and k 14 sts along left side of instep, k remaining 12 sts from left-hand needle.
2nd row: P across all sts, including 12 sts on other needle (59 sts). Starting with a k row, work 11 rows in stockinette st, then work 3 rows in garter st.
SOLE:
1st row: K 2 tog, k 25, k 2 tog, k 1, k 2 tog, k 25, k 2 tog (55 sts).
2nd and 4th rows: P across.
3rd row: K 2 tog, k 23, k 2 tog, k 1, k 2 tog, k 23, k 2 tog (51 sts).
5th row: K 2 tog, k 21, k 2 tog, k 1, k 2 tog, k 21, k 2 tog (47 sts). Bind off.
FINISHING: Sew back and sole seams. Thread ribbon through eyelet row and tie bow in front.

NORWEGIAN SLEEPER

This lovely blue sleeper is used to keep baby warm and cozy without restricting the little legs that are always kicking in the air. It is worked in an allover pattern, in Fair Isle technique, alternated by bands of hearts and flowers, in the tradition of Norwegian ski sweaters. The sleeper is worked in sport yarn in a bright scarlet pattern against a royal blue background.

SHOWN IN COLOR

SIZE: 4–8 months. Sleeper measures 9″ across chest at underarms and 25″ from shoulder to lower edge; width of lower edge is 18″.
MATERIALS: Bear Brand Spectator (100 percent orlon acrylic sport yarn), 4 (2-oz.) skeins royal blue no. 28 and 2 skeins scarlet no. 27; knitting needles, 1 pair no. 4 **or the size that will give you the correct gauge;** 2 buttons ¾″ in diameter; 2 snaps; aluminum crochet hook size E; 18″ neckline zipper.
GAUGE: In patt: 6 sts and 7 rows = 1″.
Note: This sleeper is worked in 2 colors in the Fair Isle technique. If you are not familiar with working with more than one color, make a swatch to practice, using needles and yarn as specified and check your gauge carefully. See page 81 for Fair Isle knitting, page 81 for bobbin knitting and page 18 for how to read charts.

FRONT: Starting at lower edge, with royal blue, cast on 109 sts. Starting with a p row, work 5 rows in stockinette st. Continue to work in stockinette st and starting with a 6th (k) row on chart, follow chart for design and key for colors. Work from A to B, then work from C back to A to complete the row. Work even in patt until 124th row on chart has been completed. P 1 row, k 1 row.
Next row: P 2 tog across (55 sts).

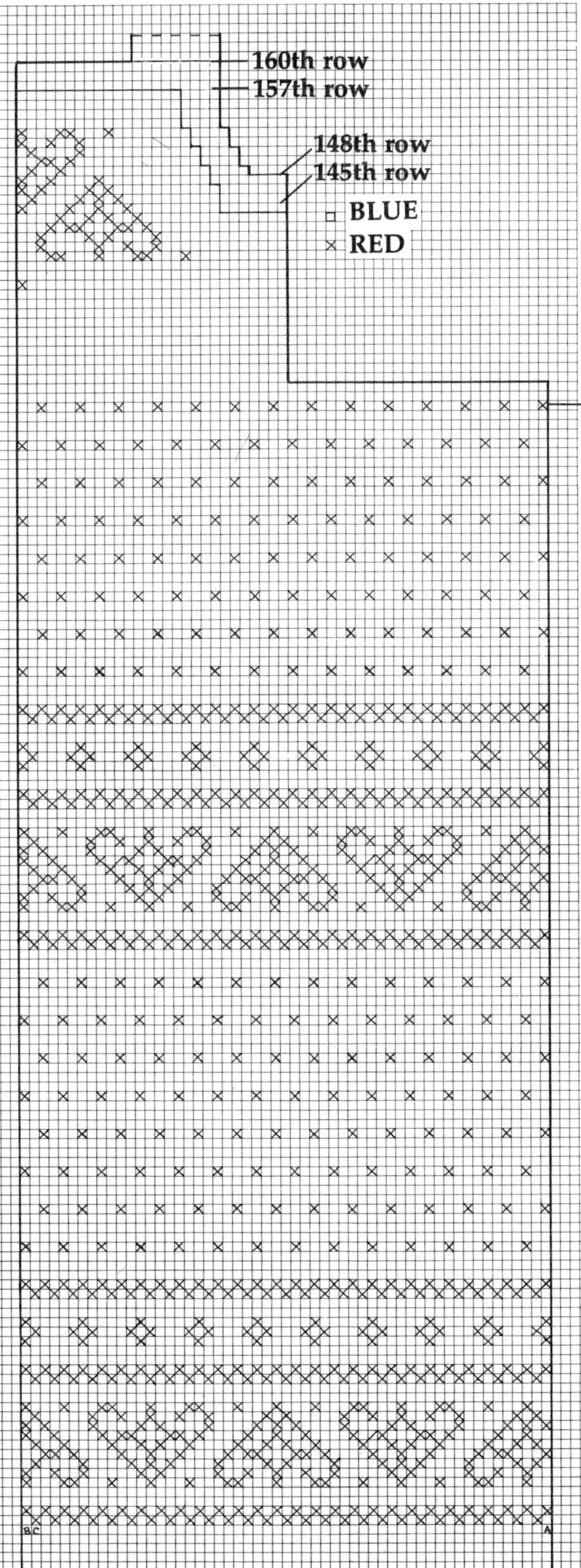
160th row
157th row
148th row
145th row
BLUE
RED
124th row
B C
A

Waistband: Work 7 rows in ribbing of k 1, p 1.
Front Bodice: Starting with a p row, follow chart until 144th row is completed, ending on wrong side.
145th row: Attach a red bobbin to work border 7 sts, continue in patt to within last 7 sts, attach another red bobbin and work last 7 border sts, continue to follow chart for patt as before, keeping border sts in red, until 148th row has been completed.
To Shape Armholes: Keeping in patt, bind off 4 sts at beg of next 2 rows, then dec 1 st at beg and end of row every other row 3 times (41 sts).

Follow chart until 157th row has been completed. Break off royal blue and continue with scarlet only, through 160th row.
To Work Straps: K across 9 sts, bind off 23 center sts, k last 9 sts. Working on these last 9 sts only in stockinette st, work even until strap measures 2¾″. Break off. Attach yarn at neck edge and work other strap to correspond.
BACK: Work same as for front, eliminating design on back bodice. Work straps to measure 3½″ instead of 2¾″.
FINISHING: Weave in all ends. Pin front and back together with right sides facing and block (see page 23), being careful to stretch ribbed waistband in the direction of the ribs so that the knit ribs lie close together for the greatest elasticity. Allow to dry thoroughly before unpinning.

With right sides together, sew front and back with back st along side seams, being careful to match patt bands. Sew snaps to straps, so that back strap closes over front strap. Sew buttons in place on right side of back strap over snap.

With crochet hk and scarlet, sc evenly around straps, armholes and neck edges.

Sew zipper in place at lower edge of sleeper.

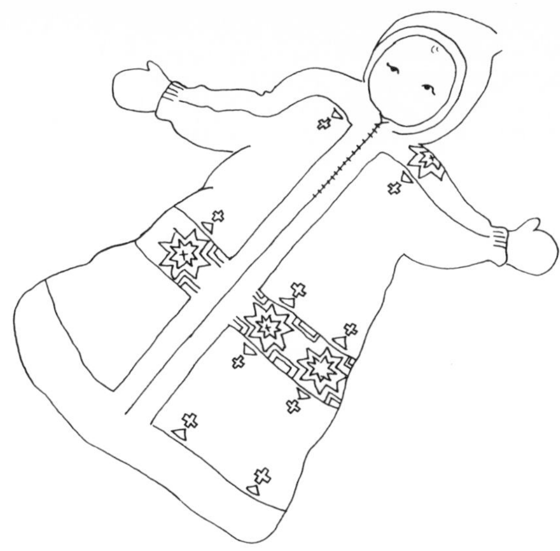

ROYAL BLUE BUNTING

Decorated in bands of red and green folk-art-inspired designs, this bunting is worked with knitting worsted in Fair Isle technique, and zips up the front. Lining is optional.

SHOWN IN COLOR

GENERAL DIRECTIONS for Royal Blue Bunting, Bunting in Geometric Design, page 66, Tweed Bunting, page 145, and Embroidered Bunting on page 152.

These four buntings are all approximately the same size. However, the chart for the knitted bunting is larger than the one for the crocheted bunting because of the difference in gauge.

LINING PATTERN: For Royal Blue Bunting and Bunting in Geometric Design (page 66), lay tracing paper over back, 1 front and hood. Draw carefully around them. Trace patterns for both buntings. For each bunting, pin paper patterns to lining fabric and cut out 2 fronts, 1 back and 1 hood, adding ½″ to all edges for seam allowance.

TO ASSEMBLE LINING: With right sides of fronts together, starting at lower edge, stitch center front seam for 4″, leaving rest of front open for zipper. With right sides of back and fronts together, stitch lower edge, sleeve, side and shoulder seams. With right sides together, fold hood rectangle crosswise, stitch seam at top edge to match bunting hood.

TO INSERT LINING: With wrong sides together, insert lining in bunting. Turn in lining edges about ½″ and sew in place at inside edge around neck opening and sleeve edges where they join cuffs. Pin side seams of lining to bunting and tack 4 or 5 times along seams. Turn in lining ½″ and slip-stitch in place along inside edge of zipper opening. With wrong sides together, insert hood lining in hood. Turn in lining edges ½″ and sew in place at inside face edge and inside edge around neck opening.

TO MAKE POMPOM: See page 25.

SIZE: Birth to 6 months. Bunting measures 15″ across back from underarm to underarm, and length from shoulder to lower edge is 25″. Sleeve length is 5¼″.

MATERIALS: Coats and Clark's Red Heart knitting worsted, 8 oz. skipper blue no. 848, 6 oz. devil red no. 903 and 4 oz. apple green no. 648; knitting needles, 1 pair no. 7 and 1 set (4) dp needles no. 5 for cuffs **or the size that will give you the correct gauge;** steel crochet hook no. 0; 20″ neckline zipper; 1¾ yds. of 36″-wide lining material such as flannel or calico-printed cotton.

GAUGE: 5 sts = 1″; 11 rows = 2″.

WORKING WITH TWO COLORS: Fair Isle Knitting, see page 81.

HOW TO READ CHARTS: See page 18.

Note: Yoke and sleeves are worked in one piece.

RIGHT FRONT: Starting at lower edge with red, cast on 47 sts. Starting with a p row, work in stockinette st for 3 rows. Continue in stockinette st and, starting with 4th row on chart, follow chart for shaping and design. Repeat from Y to Z on k rows and from Z to Y on p rows. Dec 1 st at end of 24th row (side edge). Continue to dec at side edge as indicated on chart. Work until 110th row on chart has been completed (38 sts) and piece measures about 21″ from beg, ending at side edge.

Do not break off, but continue by working sleeve and yoke in one piece as follows:

111th row: With blue, cast on 21 sts, p across (59 sts). Follow chart through 127th row.

Sleeve and Shoulder Shaping: 1st row: Bind off 14 sts for front neck, k remaining sts. Bind off.

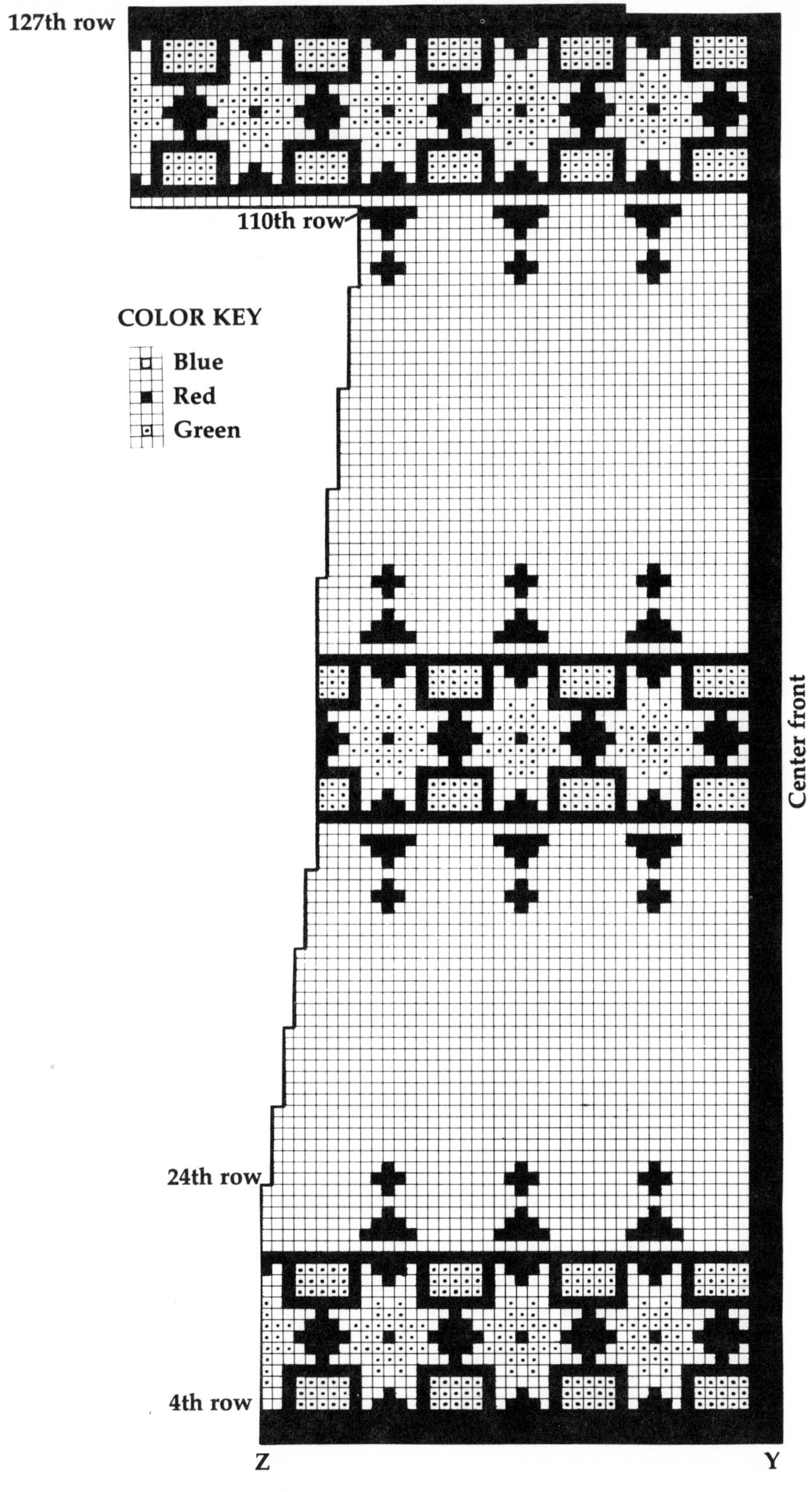

127th row

110th row

COLOR KEY

Blue

Red

Green

Center front

24th row

4th row

Z Y

LEFT FRONT: Work same as for right front, reversing patt and shapings.

BACK: There is no design on back of bunting. Starting at lower edge with blue, cast on 91 sts. Work in stockinette st and dec 1 st at beg and end of row every 2″ 9 times (73 sts). Work even until piece measures same as fronts to underarms. Do not break off yarn, but continue by working sleeves and yoke all in one piece as follows: Cast on 21 sts at beg of next 2 rows for sleeves. Work even on 115 sts until sleeves are same width as front, ending on wrong side.
Sleeve and Shoulder Shaping: 1st row: K 45, bind off 25 sts, k remaining 45 sts.
2nd row: Bind off 45 sts for top of sleeve and shoulder. Attach yarn at neck edge of opposite shoulder and bind off remaining 45 sts.

FINISHING: Weave in all ends. Pin matching pieces together and block. Allow to dry thoroughly before removing pins.
LINING PATTERN: See general directions for bunting lining. Cut hood lining after knitted hood has been completed.

TO ASSEMBLE BUNTING: Sew fronts together along center front seam for 4″ as for lining. Sew side, sleeve and shoulder seams. Sew cast-on edges at bottom of front and back together.
HOOD: With right side facing you, using red, pick up and k 70 sts around neck edge. Work 2 more rows even.
Next row: Bind off 8 sts, p across.
Following row: Bind off 8 sts, k 2, attach blue and k across to within last 3 sts, attach another ball red and k 3.

Then, keeping first and last 3 border sts in red, work even until piece measures 8″ from neck edge. Bind off.
HOOD LINING: See general directions. Fold knitted hood in half crosswise and sew bound-off edges together for top seam.
CUFFS: With red and no. 5 dp needles, pick up and k 24 sts evenly divided on 3 needles. Work even in stockinette st until cuff measures 1″ from beg. Bind off.
TRIM: With right side facing you, using crochet hk and red, work a row of sc evenly spaced along zipper opening and face edge of hood. Break off. Sew zipper in place.
TO INSERT LINING: See general directions.
TO MAKE POMPOM: See page 25.

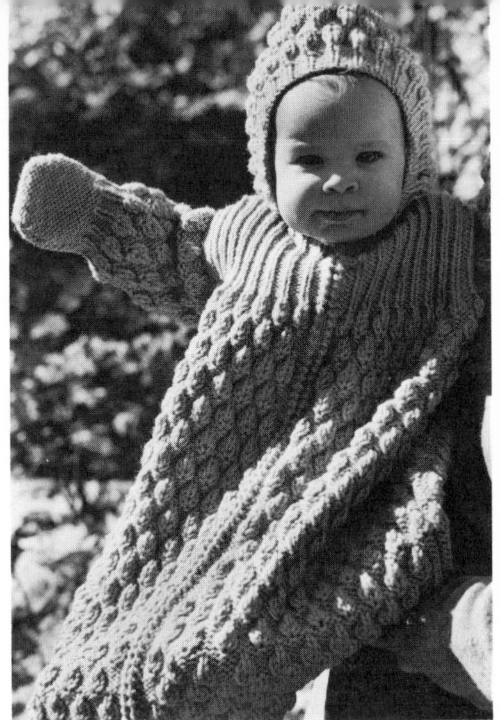

EMBOSSED BUNTING

A bunting fit for a prince. This bunting is worked in the richly embossed leaf stitch on a reverse stockinette stitch background, which gives it an almost jewelstudded texture, with a ribbed yoke, in acrylic knitting worsted weight yarn. Hood and attached mittens will keep baby snug as a bug.

SIZE: Birth to 5 months. Bunting measures 13½" across back from side seam to side seam, and 23" from shoulder to lower edge.
MATERIALS: Spinnerin Germantown de Luxe (100 percent orlon acrylic knitting worsted weight yarn), 5 (4-oz.) skeins natural no. 3284; knitting needles, 1 pair each no. 6 and no. 3 **or the size that will give you the correct gauge:** 22" neckline zipper; aluminum crochet hook, size E.
GAUGE: With no. 6 needles, 5 sts and 6 rows = 1".
EMBOSSED LEAF STITCH PATTERN: Multiple of 4 sts plus 1.
1st row (right side): P 2, * in next st work k 1, y o, k 1 (3 sts in 1 st), p 3, rep from * across, ending with p 2 instead of p 3.

2nd row: K 2, * p 3, k 3, rep from * across, ending with k 2.
3rd row: P 2, * k 3, p 3, rep from * across, ending with p 2.
4th row: Rep 2nd row.
5th row: P 2, * sl 2 tog k-wise, k 1, p2sso (2 sts dec), p 3. Rep from * across, ending with p 2.
6th row: K 2, * p 1, k 3, rep from * across, ending with k 2.
7th row: Rep 1st row, p 4 at beg and end of row, instead of p 2.
8th row: Rep 2nd row, k 4 at beg and end of row, instead of k 2.
9th row: Rep 3rd row, p 4 at beg and end of row, instead of p 2.
10th row: Rep 2nd row, k 4 at beg and end of row, instead of k 2.
11th row: Rep 5th row, p 4 at beg and end of row, instead of p 2.
12th row: Rep 6th row, k 4 at beg and end of row, instead of k 2.

Rep these 12 rows for patt.

BACK: Starting at lower edge, with no. 6 needles, cast on 93 sts. Work in patt until piece measures 21″ from beg, ending with a 6th patt row.

YOKE—FRONT: Change to no. 3 needles and dec 22 sts as follows:
1st (dec) row: P 2, * k 1, p 2 tog, p 1, rep from * across to within last 3 sts, k 1, p 2.

Establish rib patt as follows:
2nd row (wrong side): * K 2, p 1, rep from * across, ending with k 2.
3rd row: * P 2, k 1, rep from * across, ending with p 2.

Work even on these 71 sts in p 2, k 1 ribbing as established until yoke measures 3½″, ending on wrong side.
To Shape Shoulders: Bind off 11 sts at beg of next 4 rows. Place remaining 27 sts on a holder.

RIGHT FRONT: Starting at lower edge, with no. 6 needles, cast on 45 sts, work in patt as for back until piece measures 21″ from beg, ending with a 6th patt row.

YOKE—BACK: Change to no. 3 needles and work first dec row same as for back (10 sts dec—35 sts). Establish rib patt same as for back, work even on these 35 sts in p 2, k 1 ribbing

until yoke measures 3½", ending on right side (armhole edge).
To Shape Shoulder: Bind off 11 sts at beg of next 2 rows. Place remaining 13 sts on a holder.

LEFT FRONT: Work same as for right front, reversing shaping.
Note: The mittens and sleeves are worked in one piece.

MITTEN: Starting at tip of mitten with no. 3 needles, cast on 20 sts.
1st row (right side): P across.
2nd row: K across, placing a marker between 10th and 11th sts.
3rd (inc) row: P across, inc 1 st at beg and end of row, and before and after marker (4 sts inc—24 sts).

Rep 2nd and 3rd rows twice more (32 sts), slipping marker. Remove marker and work even in reverse stockinette st as established, until piece measures 2½" from beg, ending on wrong side.
Cuff: 1st row: * P 2, k 1, rep from * across, ending with p 2.
2nd row: * K 2, p 1, rep from * across, ending with k 2.

Work even in ribbing as established for 1", ending on wrong side.

SLEEVE: Change to no. 6 needles. Increase and establish patt as follows:
1st (inc) row: P 2, * in next st work k 1, y o, k 1, inc 1 st in next st, p 1, rep from * across to within last 2 sts, p 2 (9 sts inc).

Starting with a 2nd patt row, work even in patt until 36 patt rows have been completed. Bind off.

HOOD: Starting at back edge with no. 6 needles, cast on 81 sts. Work 30 rows in patt as for back. Change to no. 3 needles, then work first dec row of back yoke, establish rib patt same as for back yoke, and work 1" even in p 2, k 1 ribbing. Bind off in ribbing.

Sew shoulder seams, matching ribs.
Neck Edge: Being careful to keep in rib patt as established, work 13 sts of right front from holder, work 27 sts of back, work 13 sts of left front (53 sts), work 1" even. Bind off in ribbing.
FINISHING:
Assembling: Sew sleeves in place along side of back and front yoke. Sew mitten, underarm and side seams. Sew center front

seam for 2½″, starting at lower edge, leaving rest of front open for zipper. Sew lower edges together; sew zipper in place.

Fold hood in half crosswise and sew back seam. Sew hood to neck edge, leaving 1″ free at each front.

Trim: With right side of work facing you, starting at right front neck edge, work 1 row of reverse sc (see page 32), evenly spaced along zipper opening.

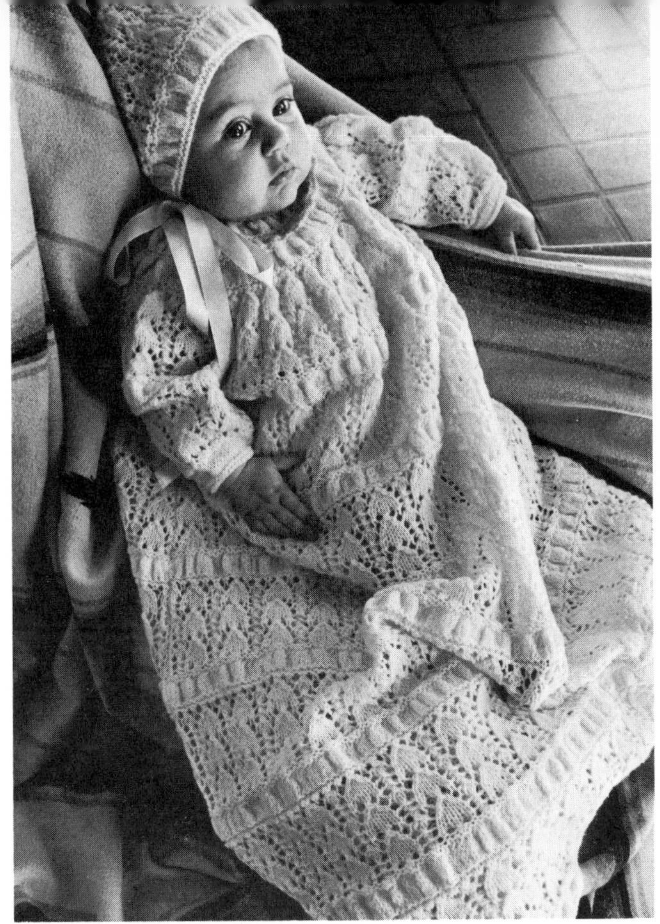

CHRISTENING DRESS AND BONNET

Truly a labor of love, this long, frothy christening dress is in a delicate snowdrop pattern, alternated with rows of ruching, in a fine ecru acrylic baby yarn, with matching bonnet. This is a project for the more experienced knitter.

SIZE: Infant. Robe measures 12″ across chest from side seam to side seam; length from center back neck to lower edge is 30″. Sleeve length is 5¾″.
MATERIALS: Brunswick Delf-baby (100% acrylic) yarn, 11 (1-oz.) skeins ecru no. 12000; knitting needles, 1 pair no. 4 **or the**

size that will give you the correct gauge; 3 buttons, 3⁄8″ in diameter; 5 yds. 1⁄2″-wide satin ribbon; 1 set (4) dp needles, no. 4; 1 steel crochet hook, no. 0.
GAUGE: In patt 13 sts = 2″; 9 rows = 1″.

DRESS

RUCHING PATTERN: Multiple of 8 sts plus 5 sts.
1st row (wrong side) through 3rd row: K across.
4th row: K, increasing 1 st in each st across.
5th through 8th rows: Starting with a p row, work in stockinette st.
9th row: P 2 tog across.
10th row: P across.
11th row: K across.
SNOWDROP LACE PATTERN:
12th row (right side): K 1, * y o, sl 1, k 2 tog, psso, y o, k 1. Rep from * across.
13th and all uneven rows: P across.
14th and 16th rows: K 1, * y o, sl 1 p-wise, k 2 tog, psso, y o, k 5. Rep from * across, ending with k 1 instead of k 5.
18th row: K 4, * y o, sl 1, k 1, psso, k 1, k 2 tog, y o, k 3. Rep from * across, ending with k 4 instead of k 3.
20th row: Rep 12th row.

Rep 13th through 20th rows twice more.

Rep these 36 rows for patt (1 band of ruching and 3 bands of snowdrop lace).

FRONT: Starting at lower edge, cast on 141 sts. Work even in patt until 2 bands of ruching and 3 bands of snowdrop lace have been completed in all, ending with an 11th patt row. Dec 1 st at beg and end of next row (12th patt of snowdrop lace), then every inch twice more (135 sts), being careful to continue in patt as established. Then work 1 band of ruching even, ending with an 11th patt row. Continue to dec in this manner (dec on snowdrop bands only) until 117 sts remain, ending with a 20th patt row. Continue to work even in patt until 7 bands of ruching and 18 bands of snowdrop lace have been completed in all. Starting with a 12th patt row, work 13 rows even in snowdrop lace pattern, ending with a 16th patt row.
To Shape Armholes: Bind off 5 sts at beg of next 2 rows. Dec 1 st at beg and end of next row, then every other row 4 times more. Work 1 row even (97 sts). Place these sts on a holder.

BACK: Work same as for front, dec 1 st on last k row (96 sts). To divide for back neck opening, place 48 sts each on 2 holders.

SLEEVES: Starting at lower edge, cast on 39 sts.
1st row (wrong side) through 3rd row: K across.
4th through 9th row: Starting with a k row, work in stockinette st.
10th row: P across.
11th row: K inc 14 sts evenly spaced (53 sts). Starting with a 12th patt row, work 3 bands of snowdrop lace and 1 band of ruching, then starting with a 12th patt row, work 13 rows of snowdrop lace pattern, ending with a 16th patt row.
To Shape Armholes: Work same as for back (33 sts).

YOKE: Hold dp needle in left hand and, with wrong side of work facing you, slip pieces onto it in the following order: 48 sts of left back, 33 sts of sleeve, 97 sts of front, 33 sts of second sleeve and 48 sts of right back (259 sts).
1st row (wrong side): K across.
2nd row: K 2 tog across (130 sts).
3rd row: K across.
4th row: K across, inc 1 st in each st.
5th through 9th rows: Starting with a p row, work in stockinette st.
10th row: K 2 tog across.
11th row: K across.
12th row: K, dec 20 sts as evenly spaced as possible across row (110 sts).
13th row: K across.

Rep 4th through 13th rows once more (90 sts). Then rep 4th through 13th rows again, dec 25 sts on 12th row (65 sts). K 4 rows even. Bind off.

FINISHING: Sew side, sleeve and underarm seams. With right side of work facing you, work 1 row of sc along back neck opening. Break off. Starting at upper corner of right back, attach yarn, * ch 3 to form button loop, sk 2 sc, sc in each sc for 1″, rep from * twice more (3 button loops made), work to end of opening. Break off. Sew buttons along left back edge opposite button loops.

BONNET

Starting at front edge, cast on 72 sts. Work ruching as follows:
1st row (wrong side) through 3rd row: K across.
4th row: K across, inc 1 st in each st.
5th through 9th rows: Starting with a p row, work in stockinette st.
10th row: K 2 tog across.
11th row: K across.
12th row: K across, inc 13 sts evenly spaced (85 sts).
13th row: K across.

Starting with a 12th patt row (right side), work 3 snowdrop lace bands as before. K 3 rows, dec 5 sts evenly spaced across second k row (80 sts).
To Shape Cap, 1st row: * K 8, k 2 tog, rep from * across.
2nd and all even-numbered rows: P across.
3rd row: * K 7, k 2 tog. Rep from * across.
5th row: * K 6, k 2 tog. Rep from * across.

Continue in this manner, dec 8 sts every other row until 16 sts remain. P 1 row.
Next row: K 2 tog across. Break off, leaving a 10″ end of yarn. Thread this end into a sewing needle and run through remaining 8 sts. Draw up tightly and break off. Sew neck edges of cap together from this point downward for 3″.
Casing: With right side of work facing you, pick up and k 40 sts along lower edge. K 2 rows even.
3rd row: K 2, * y o, k 2 tog. Rep from * across, ending with y o, k 2. K 2 rows even. Bind off. Run ribbon for ties through casing. Sew bows at sides.

Sewn and Embroidered Clothes

SEWING

What a pleasant way to spend your time, sewing these little garments. They are easy to make and take little time and fabric.

There are many practical fabrics to choose from these days—cotton blends, knits or terry cloth—none of which need ironing.

All the designs have simple shapes, but you can decorate them to your heart's content with embroidery, braid, ribbons, rickrack, eyelet or lace.

Here are just some of the projects: buntings to sew and embroider, tops, kimono and dress made of bandanna handkerchiefs, a luxurious bath set made of velour towels, a quilted liner for the bassinet and much more.

TECHNIQUES:

Before you embark on a project, read the sections on how to enlarge the patterns to actual size (page 22) and cutting and sewing your patterns (page 22).

Make sure your fabric and pattern pieces are smooth and flat. Carefully lay out the pattern pieces on the fabric, following such instructions as "place on fold," "cut 2 . . ." etc. Make sure to place patterns on the straight grain of the fabric in the direction of the arrow. Always fold fabric with right side on the inside and cut pattern on the wrong side.

Keep pattern pinned to fabric to cut. Unpin and follow specific sewing directions. ½" seam allowance is included in all patterns unless indicated otherwise.

Here are the explanations of the most commonly used sewing terms:

Selvages: The finished edges of the fabric.

On the Straight Grain: When the arrow on a pattern piece is parallel to a selvage.

On the Fold: Fabric may be folded double to cut 2 sections at once. Or, when only 1 pattern half is given of a section, which you need in 1 piece, the pattern is placed on the fold. Cut and you have the complete piece.

Basting: To handsew 2 pieces together temporarily.

Gathering: Pulling a piece of fabric together along a line of running stitches.
Slip Stitching: An invisible way of finishing hems or facings.
Trimming: Cutting away excess fabric—for example, to make a seam allowance narrower after sewing it, to eliminate bulkiness. It also means "decorating with . . ."

EMBROIDERY

Just a little bit of embroidery can give your handmade garment that special finishing touch.

When an embroidery design is given, first enlarge the design to the actual size (see page 22 on how to do this). Then trace it on tracing paper or tissue paper and transfer it to the item to be embroidered by tracing it over dressmaker's carbon, being careful not to smear the fabric.

Always use embroidery thread in proportion to the background material you are working on. For example, when embroidering a knitted or crocheted garment, use matching weight yarn.

When working on cotton flannel or lightweight cottons, use 3 strands of embroidery floss; on heavier fabric, use the full 6 strands or crewel yarns.

See the pages listed below for diagrams showing you how to execute the basic embroidery stitches:

Cross-stitch, 74
Star stitch, 153
Satin stitch, 153
Stem or outline stitch, 153
Lazy daisy, 153
French knot, 153
Blanket or buttonhole stitch, 153
Roman stitch, 153
Tent stitch, 147

BATH CAPE AND WASH MITTEN

What could be more inviting than this soft, velvety bath cape to wrap baby in? Cape consists of one pink velour towel and 2 washcloths for hood. Wash mitten is made of one washcloth. All are trimmed with gingham rick-rack and eyelet ruffle.

MATERIALS: 1 velour pink towel, 23″ x 41½″; 3 washcloths, each 12″ square; 2½ yds. of rickrack; 2½″ yds. of 1¼″-wide eyelet trim; 1 yd. of ⅝″-wide satin ribbon.

CAPE

Sewing: Note: Make ½″ seams. For hood section: With right sides together, stitch 2 washcloths together along 1 side. Press seam open.

Gather one long side of towel to measure 23″, leaving 2″ at each side free.

With right sides together, sew gathered edge of towel and long edge of hood section together. Sew top seam of hood, with right sides together.

Along front edges and hood, fold 1″ under to wrong side. Stitch. On right side, baste eyelet trim in place 1″ in from edge along front opening and hood. Stitch rickrack in place over basting line. Sew an 18″ ribbon tie to each side of hood.

MITTEN

Fold under 1″ along one side of washcloth to wrong side. Stitch. Baste eyelet trim to mitten on right side, 1″ in from folded edge. Stitch rickrack in place over basting line. Fold in half with right sides together and stitch remaining 2 sides, leaving trimmed side open.

THREE-PIECE QUILTED CALICO SET

What could be more American than calico and gingham? But quilted and fastened in Chinese-peasant style, this set combines the best of both worlds. Turned-up cuffs show the bright inside on all three pieces.

SHOWN IN COLOR

SIZE: Birth to 3 months. Jacket measures 9½″ across at underarms, 10½″ from shoulder to lower edge. Sleeve length is 2½″ with cuff turned up. Bonnet measures 13″ along face edge, 6″ across top seam. Booties measure 4″ from heel to toe.
MATERIALS: 1 yd. of 45″-wide quilted printed cotton; 1 yd. of 45″-wide gingham for lining; 2 (5-yd.) packages of double-fold bias tape.

JACKET

CUTTING: Enlarge pattern and cut fabric (see page 22). For jacket back, cut 1 piece on fold; for front, cut 2 pieces.

For lining, cut same pieces as for jacket.

SEWING: For jacket, with right sides facing, stitch fronts and back together at shoulders and sleeve seams. Stitch side seams to within 2½″ from lower edge for side slits. Press open seams.

For lining, sew as for jacket. Trim seams. With wrong sides together, insert lining into jacket. Baste in place, matching raw edges.

Treating both layers of fabric as one, bind neck, front, lower and sleeve edges and side slits with bias tape.

Cut four 7″ lengths of bias tape, fold lengthwise and stitch.

Sew 2 ties to right front edge, the first one 5½″ from lower edge, the other 3″ below the first one.

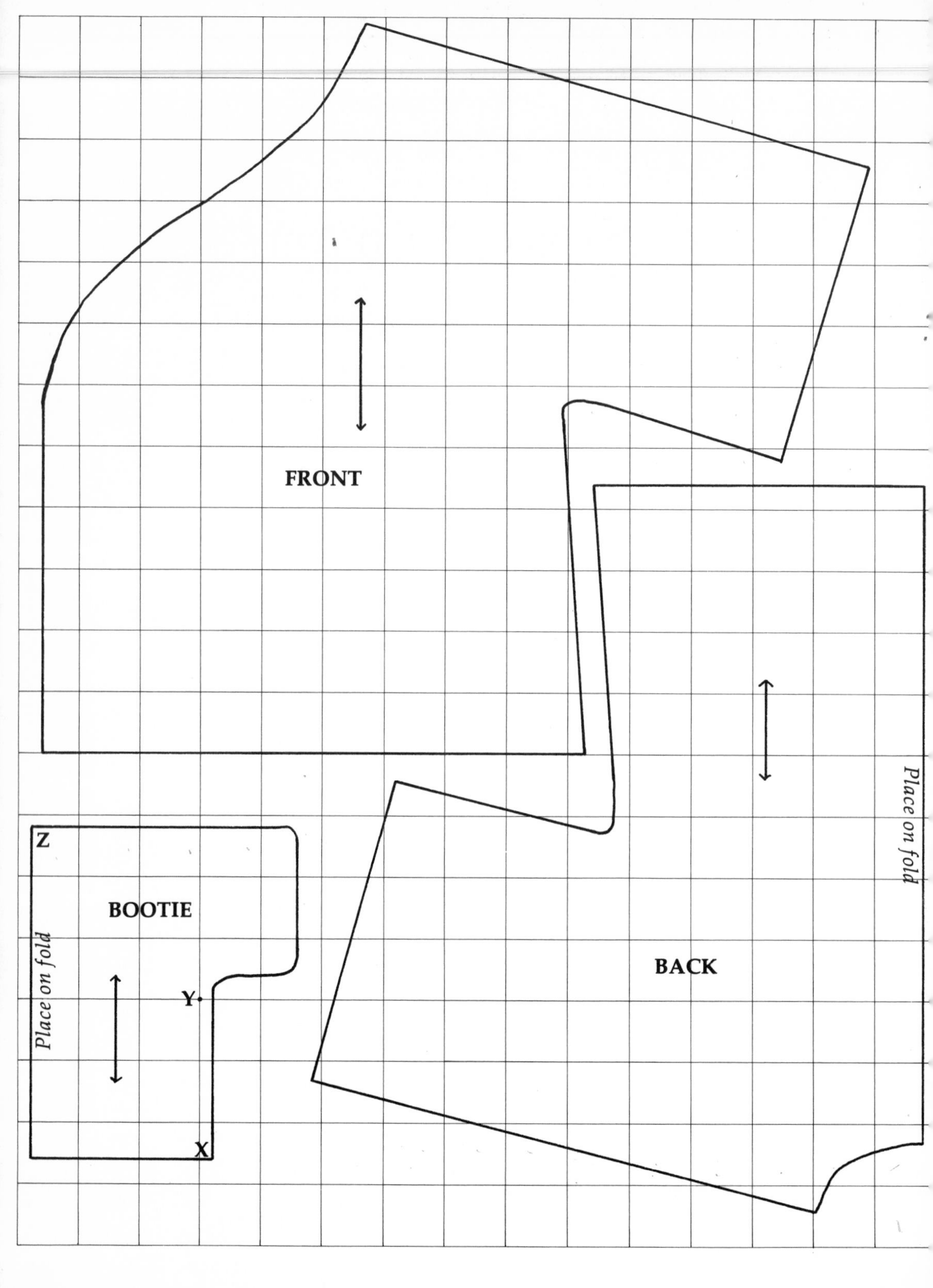
FRONT
BACK
Place on fold
Z
BOOTIE
Place on fold
Y
X

Sew 2 ties to correspond on opposite side, 6½″ in from left front edge. Turn up cuffs.

HAT

Cut one 7″ x 14″ rectangle each of quilted cotton and lining. Fold each piece in half crosswise. Stitch center back seam on each piece. Press open seams; trim lining seam. With wrong sides facing, insert lining into hat. Baste lining to hat, treating 2 layers as one. Bind front edge with bias tape.

Turn front edge 1¼″ back to right side for cuff. Baste cuff in place at neck edge. Gather neck edge slightly to measure 9″. Bind neck edge, extending ends of tape 7″ for ties.

BOOTIES

Cut 2 pieces each of quilted cotton and lining fabric. Fold all pieces in half lengthwise. Stitch foot, toe and sole seams, from Y to Z on pattern, leaving X to Y open. Trim all seams. With wrong sides together, insert lining into booties. Baste along top edge and front opening. Bind top edge and front opening with bias tape.

QUILTED AND RUFFLED LINER

This will transform any ordinary laundry basket into a comfy bassinet. Of course, you can dress up a standard bassinet in the same manner.

SHOWN IN COLOR

MATERIALS:
Note: No specific yardage has been given since the size of baskets and bassinets may vary. 45″-wide solid or printed quilted cotton; ¾″-wide bias tape; round elastic. See page 22 for cutting and sewing.
CUTTING: For liner, cut a strip of fabric the length of the circumference of the basket, by the depth of the basket measured from top edge to floor. Add 1″ seam allowance all around. You may have to piece the fabric to obtain the necessary dimensions. (Example: circumference is 80″, depth is 16″; cut a strip 82″ x 18″.)

For ruffle, cut a strip 1¾ times the circumference of basket, by the depth of the ruffle you want, adding 1″ seam allowance all around. (Example: circumference is 80″, depth of ruffle is 7″; cut a strip 142″ x 9″.)
SEWING: With right sides facing, stitch narrow ends of liner strip together. Press open seam.

With right sides facing, stitch narrow ends of ruffle strip together. Press open seam.

Gather ruffle to fit around liner. With right sides facing, matching raw edges, stitch ruffle and liner together, allowing for openings if your laundry basket has handles. Trim.
Casing: Turn lower edge of liner 1″ to wrong side. Baste along fold, turn under raw edge ¼″ and stitch, leaving an opening to insert elastic.
To Finish Ruffle: Bind as follows: hold right side of tape fac-

ing wrong side of ruffle, matching raw edges. Stitch. Turn tape to right side of ruffle, press and topstitch in place.

Cut elastic the length of circumference of inside bottom of basket. Run elastic through casing and knot ends together.

BRIGHT BANDANNAS

Pretty bandannas can be made into four charming tops—a kimono, a dress, a shirt and a sundress. You can make them in a couple of hours using one or two 22/24″ square bandannas. Don't worry if the bandannas are an inch or so smaller or larger; the designs are quite roomy to begin with.

Of course, any leftover piece of pretty fabric in these sizes may be used.

BANDANNA SHIRT.

SIZE: 3–6 months. Shirt measures 11½″ across from side seam to side seam, 11″ from shoulder to lower edge. Sleeve length is 5″.

MATERIALS: One 24″-square red bandanna; 1 (5-yd.) package double-fold bias tape to match.

CUTTING: Enlarge pattern (see page 22). Fold bandanna in half lengthwise, then fold in half again crosswise. Cut fabric according to diagram, adding ½″ seam allowance to sleeve edge, underarm edge, side edge and lower edge. You are cut-

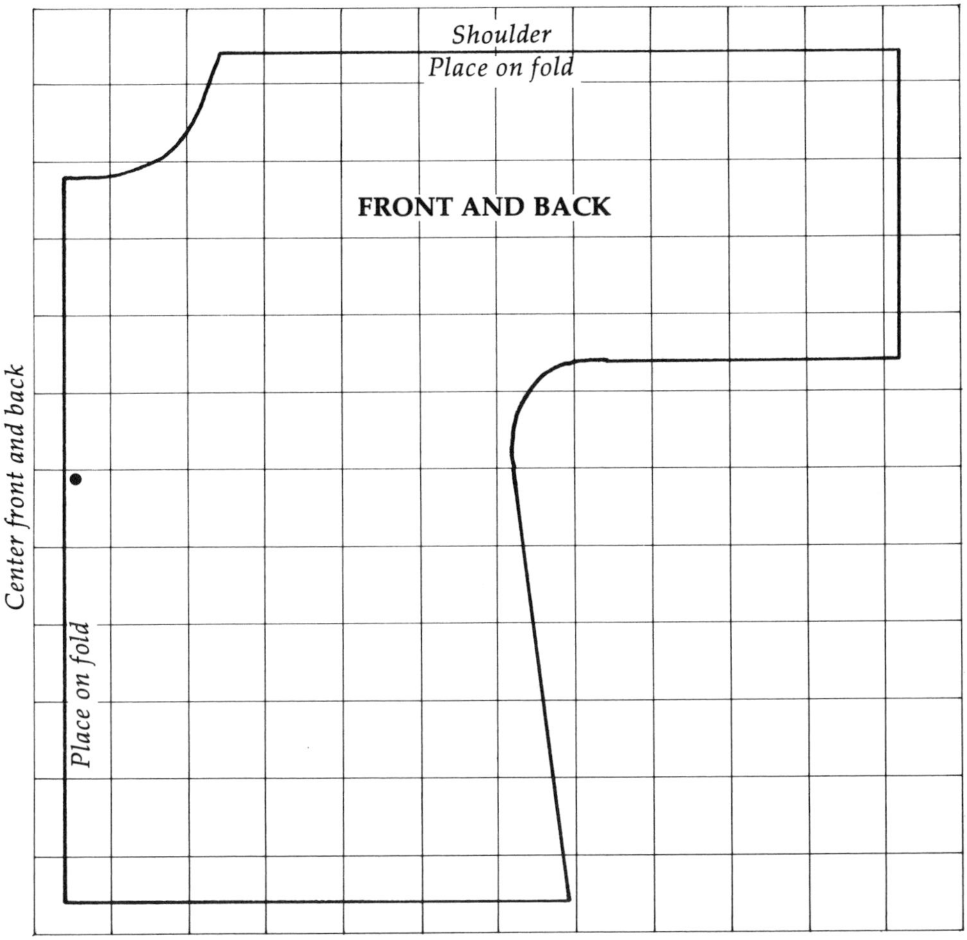

Shoulder
Place on fold
FRONT AND BACK
Center front and back
Place on fold

Shoulder fold
Center front fold
X

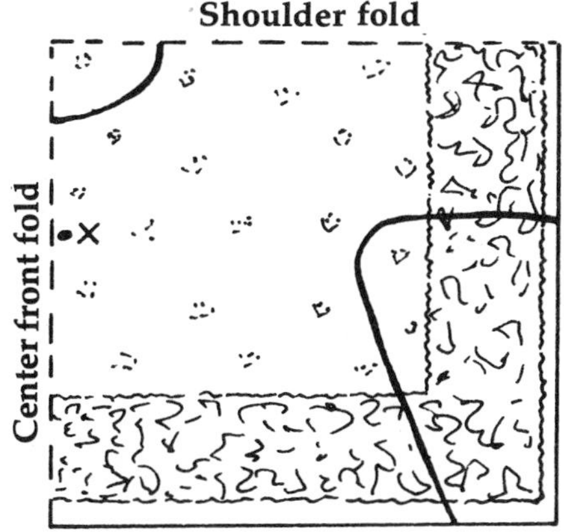

ting front and back at the same time. Cut through one center fold to X to form back opening.

SEWING: With right sides together, sew sleeve and side seams. Make a narrow hem along lower edge and at sleeve edges.

Bind neck edge and back opening with bias tape. Cut four 7½″ lengths of bias tape for ties, fold them lengthwise and stitch.

Sew 2 ties to left back neck opening, first one at top, the second 1¾″ below it.

Sew ties to correspond to opposite side.

A WHIMSICAL VARIATION

Make a shirt of muslin or fine cotton in the same manner as the bandanna shirt on page 132, but bind wrist edges and lower edge with bias tape as well.

Enlarge the embroidery design (see page 22) and transfer it (see page 124) to the front of the shirt—or a bib, for that matter—following drawing for position. Work the design completely in satin stitch, using 3 strands of embroidery floss.

These motifs were copied from ancient petroglyphs, stone carvings by the Taino Indians, the original inhabitants of Puerto Rico, who attributed great magical powers to these human and animal symbols.

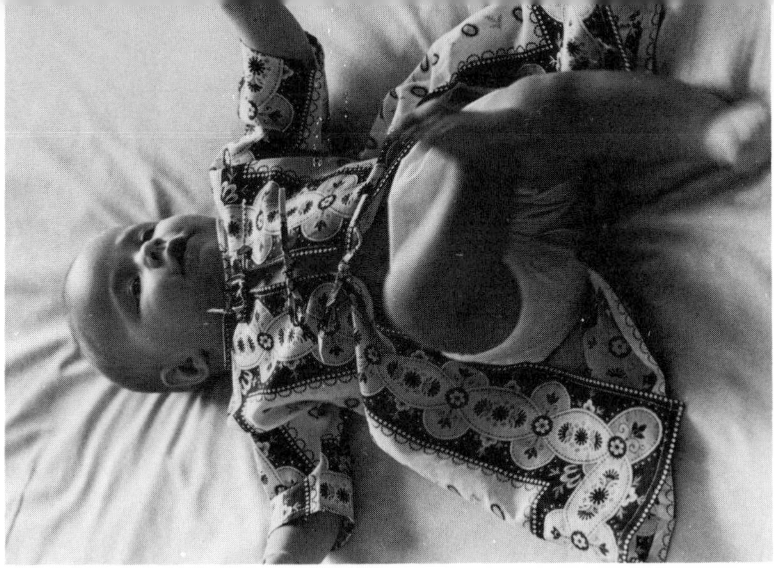

BLUE BANDANNA KIMONO

SIZE: Birth to 6 months. Kimono measures 11½″ across back at underarms, 20½″ from shoulder to lower edge. Sleeve length is 4″.

MATERIALS: Two 24″-square blue bandannas; 1 (5-yd.) package double bias tape to match (or contrasting).

CUTTING: Enlarge pattern on next page (see p. 22). Fold bandannas in half. Cut fabric according to diagram below, adding ½″ seam allowance to all edges except front edge and neck edge.

For back, cut 1 piece on fold; for front, cut 2 pieces.

SEWING: With right sides together, sew shoulder seams, sleeve and side seams. Sew a narrow hem along lower edge and wrist edges. Bind neck and front edges with bias tape. Cut eight 7½″ lengths of bias tape for ties. Fold them lengthwise and stitch. Sew 4 ties to left front edge, first one at neck edge, the others 2″ apart. Sew 4 ties to correspond on opposite side.

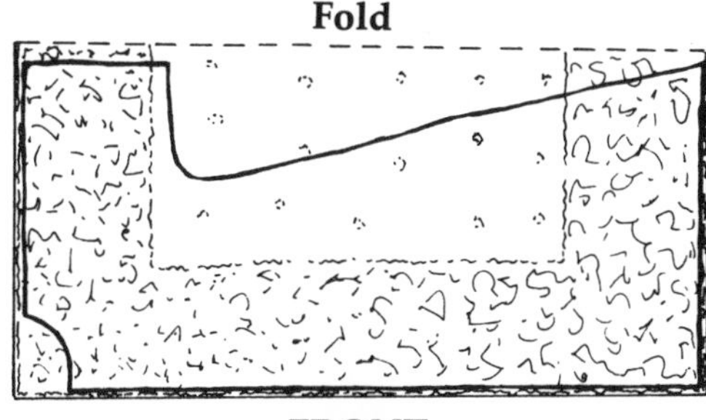

FRONT

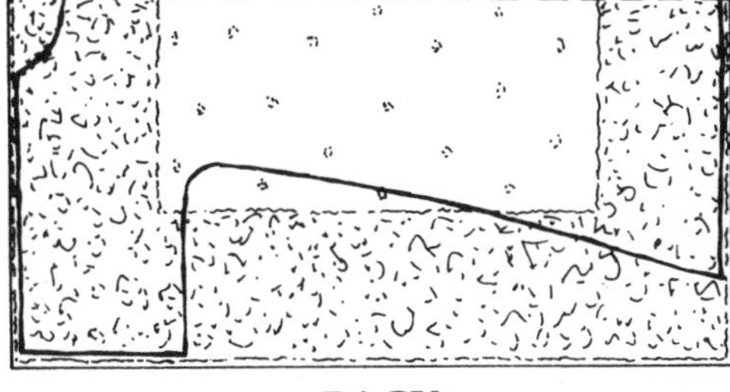

BACK

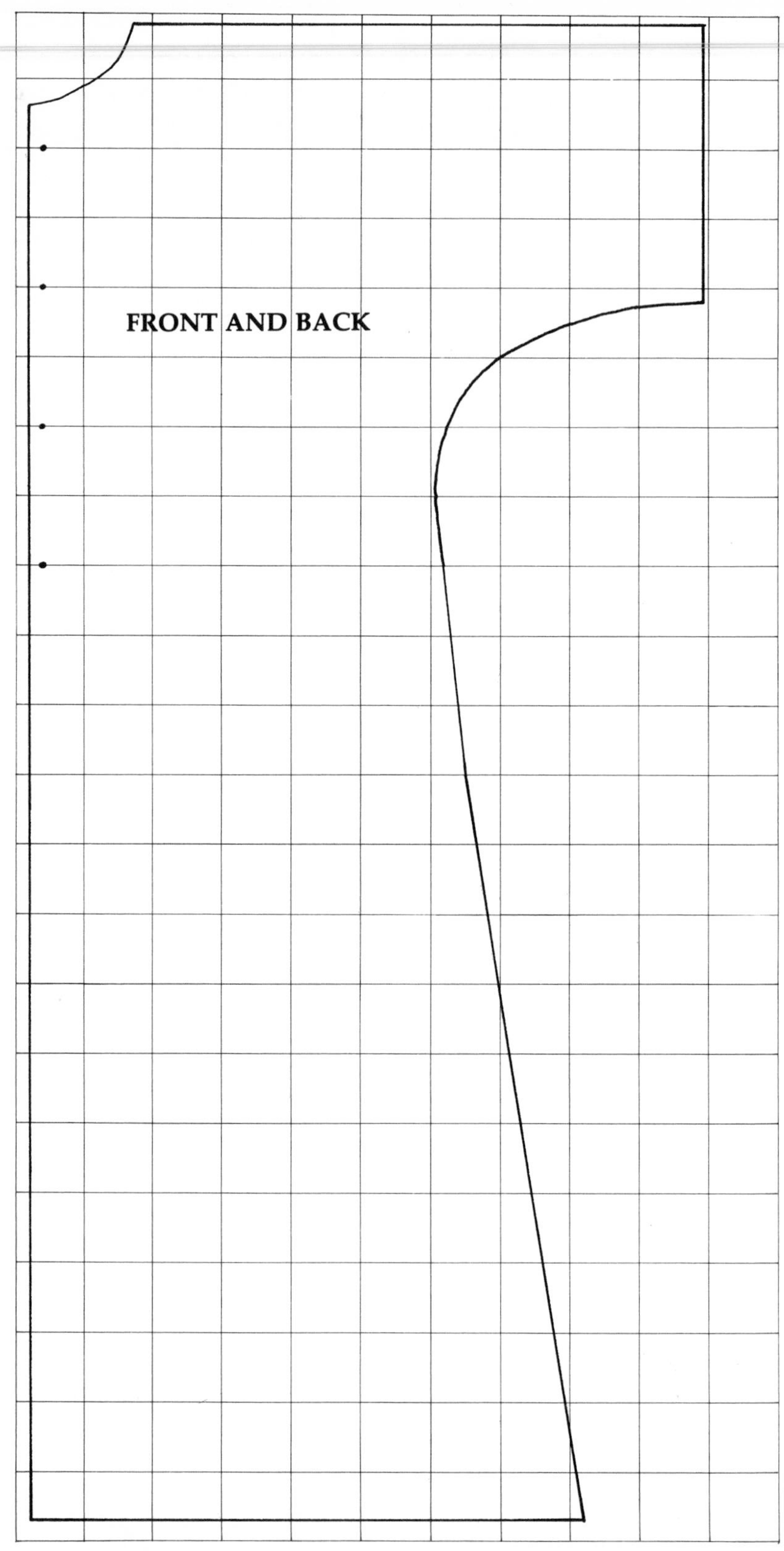
FRONT AND BACK

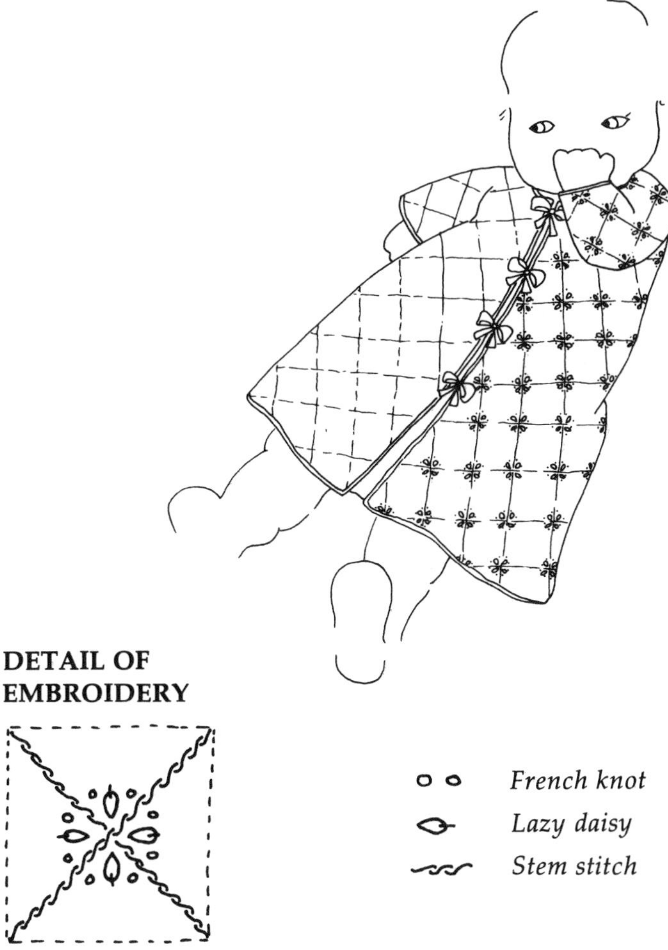

P.S. A QUILTED ROBE

Using Blue Bandanna Kimono pattern, make a cozy long robe, a short jacket or sleeveless vest out of red quilted cotton.

Using 3 strands of yellow embroidery floss, embroider in stem stitch over all the stitching lines of quilting. Where lines cross, work a little flower in lazy-daisy stitch and 2 French knots in each of 4 corners, alternating peacock blue and emerald green embroidery thread.

Bind as for kimono, with matching yellow bias tape (binding lower edge and wrist edge also).

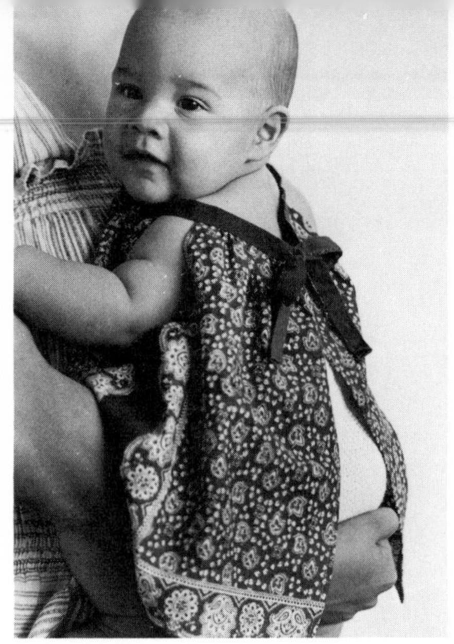

BANDANNA SUNDRESS

SIZE: 9–12 months. Dress measures 18″ around chest at underarms, 12″ from center front neck edge to lower edge.

MATERIALS: Two 20″-square blue bandannas; 1 (5-yd.) package double bias tape.

CUTTING: Enlarge pattern (see page 22). Fold bandannas in half. Cut fabric according to diagram. For front, cut 1 piece on fold; for back, cut 1 piece on fold. Cut fold for back opening. Cut a strip (piece if necessary) 40″ x 1½″ of leftover fabric.

SEWING: Sew side seams. Bind armholes and back opening with bias tape. Sew a narrow hem along lower edge.

Gather front to measure 6¼″, and left and right back sections to measure 3″ each.

On strip leave 11″ free at each end for ties, and 2″ for each armhole opening between backs and front.

With right sides together, sew dress to strip. Fold strip in half to wrong side, turn raw edge under ¼″ and slip-stitch in place over seam and across armhole opening. Tie in back.

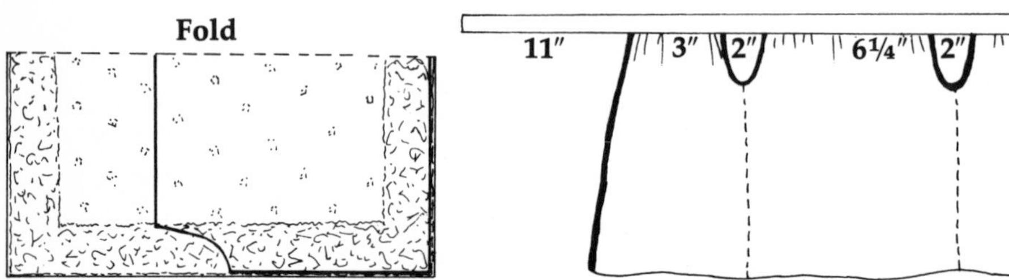

FRONT AND BACK

Place on fold

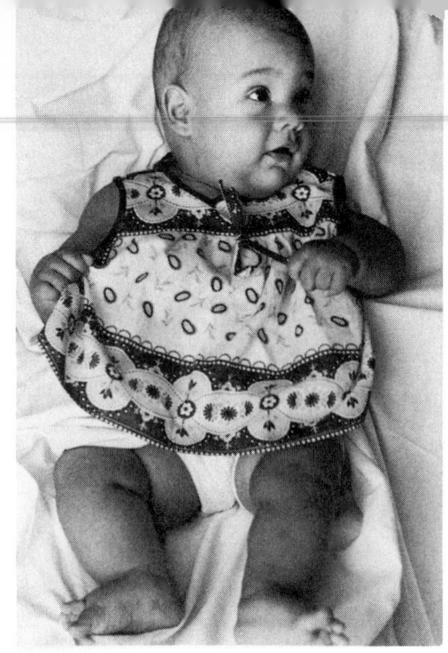

BANDANNA DRESS

SIZE: 6–12 months. Dress measures 13½″ across at underarms, 11½″ from shoulder to lower edge. Skirt length is 8¼″.

MATERIALS: Two 24″-square red bandannas; 1 package double bias tape; 2 snaps.

CUTTING: Enlarge pattern (see page 22). Fold bandannas in half. Cut fabric following diagram. For front yoke, cut 1 piece on fold; for back, cut 2 pieces.

For front skirt, cut 1 piece on fold; for back skirt, cut 2 pieces.

SEWING: With right sides of fabric together, sew shoulder seams of yoke and side seams of skirt.

Gather upper edge of front skirt to measure 9″, and each back section to measure 5½″.

With right sides together and raw edges matching, pin skirt front to yoke front, and skirt back sections to yoke back sections. Stitch seams and trim.

Turn under back edges ¼″, stitch. Sew a narrow hem along lower edge of skirt. Then fold back edges to inside along fold lines to form facing. Tack at bodice seam.

With bias tape, bind neck edge and armhole edges. Cut one 14″ length of bias tape for bow, fold it lengthwise and stitch. Tie a bow and tack to center front bodice seam. Sew 2 snaps at back bodice edge.

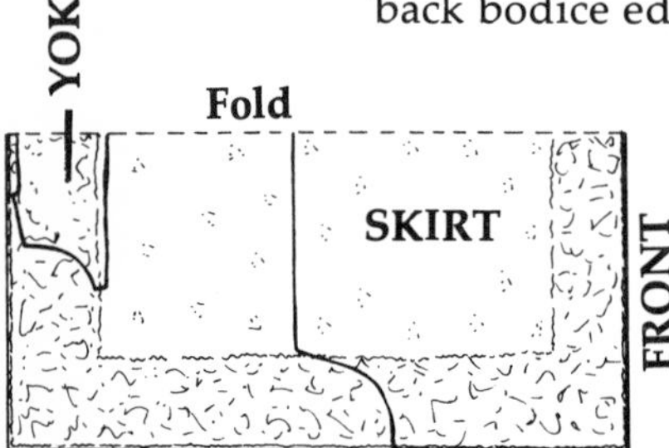

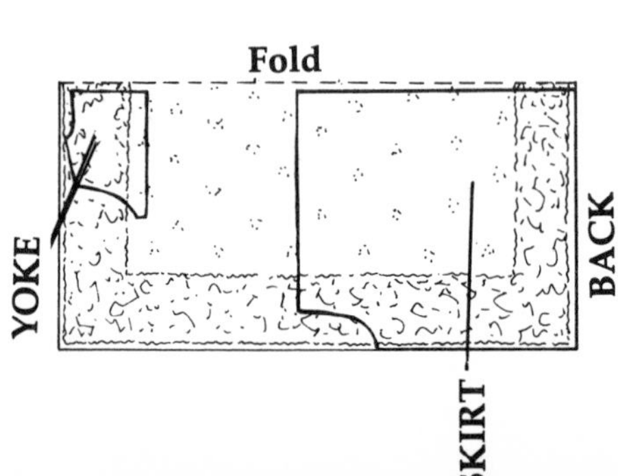

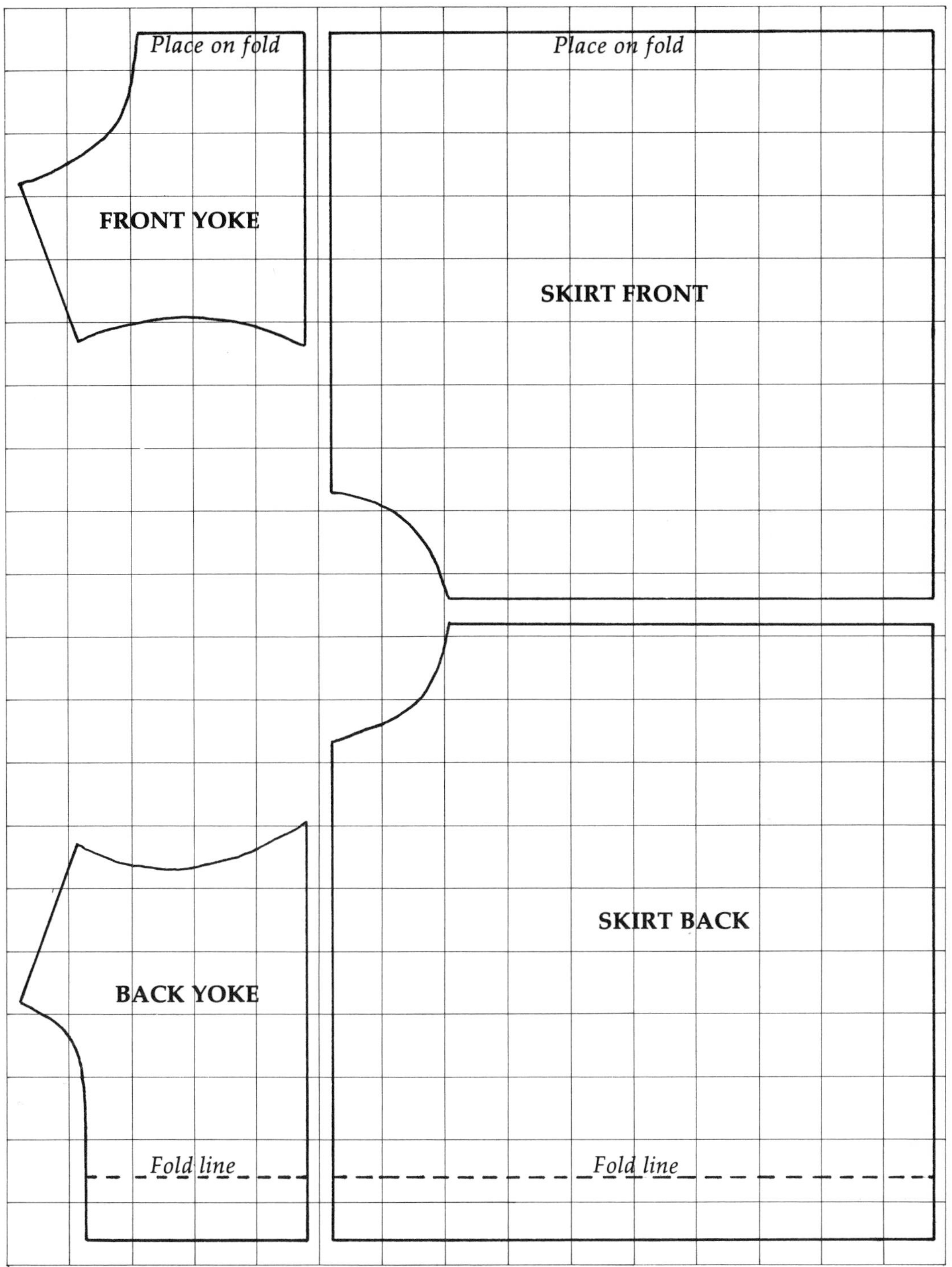
Place on fold
FRONT YOKE
Place on fold
SKIRT FRONT
SKIRT BACK
BACK YOKE
Fold line
Fold line

SWISS SMOCK

A bright blue cotton top, with dropped shoulder line and gathers at center back neck is trimmed in red braid and yellow rickrack. This smock is inspired by the smocks worn by shepherd boys who tend the sheep high in the summery Swiss Alps.

SHOWN IN COLOR

SIZE: 1 year. Smock measures 13½″ across at underarms for a loose fit, 11½″ from shoulder to lower edge. Sleeve length is 4″.

MATERIALS: ¾ yd. of 45″-wide royal blue cotton-polyester fabric; 2½ yds. yellow rickrack; 3¾ yds. of ¼″-wide braid or ribbon.

CUTTING: Enlarge pattern (see page 22). For back cut 1 piece on fold, for front cut 2 pieces. Cut 2 sleeves and 2 pockets, and 2 pieces for neck facing.

SEWING: Stitch center front seam for 5½″ starting at lower edge; press open seam.

Gather top edges of each front section between dots to measure 4″. Gather back neck section between dots to measure 3″. With right sides together and raw edges matching, sew front sections to back along dropped shoulder line.

With right sides together, raw edges matching, sew sleeves in place between Xs.

Sew center back neck seam of facing; press seam open. Turn under raw edges ¼″, stitch. Leave center front edges unfinished. With right sides together, sew facing to neck edge. Trim and clip where necessary. Turn facing to inside of smock and press. Sew a narrow hem along lower edge and sleeve edges and top edges of pockets.

Following drawing, sew trimming in place, positioning the braid over half the width of the rickrack, along lower edges,

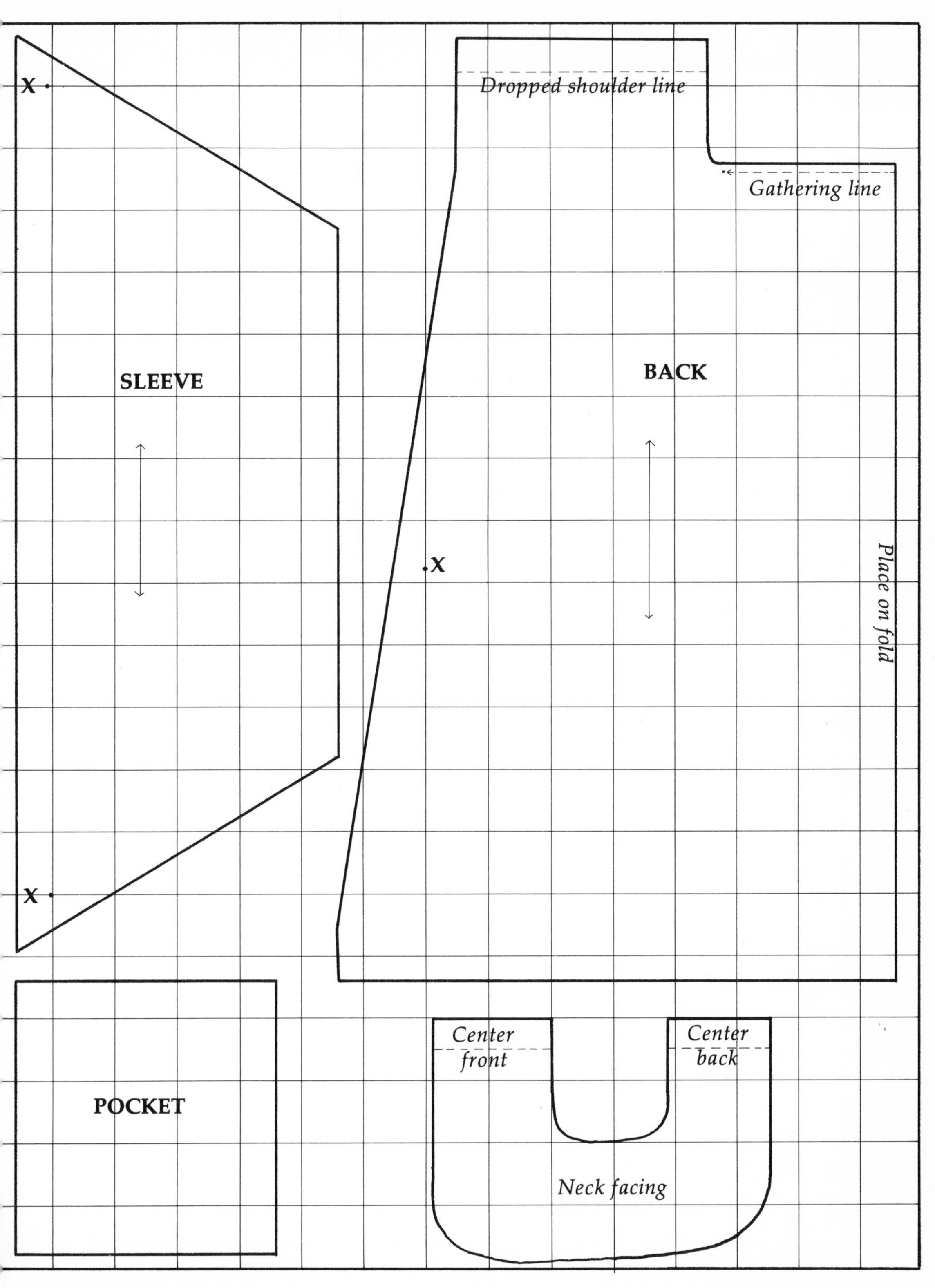

X
X
SLEEVE
X
X
Dropped shoulder line
Gathering line
BACK
Place on fold
POCKET
Center front
Center back
Neck facing

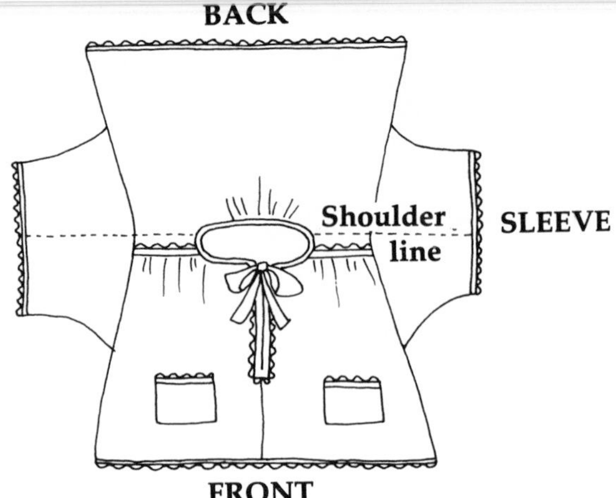

sleeve edges, dropped shoulder seam, front neck opening and along top edge of pockets.

Sew braid only around neck edge, extending ends of braid 11″ for ties.

Turn under raw edges ¼″ on remaining 3 sides of each pocket. Following drawing for position, stitch in place.

With right sides together, sew sleeve and side seams.

X

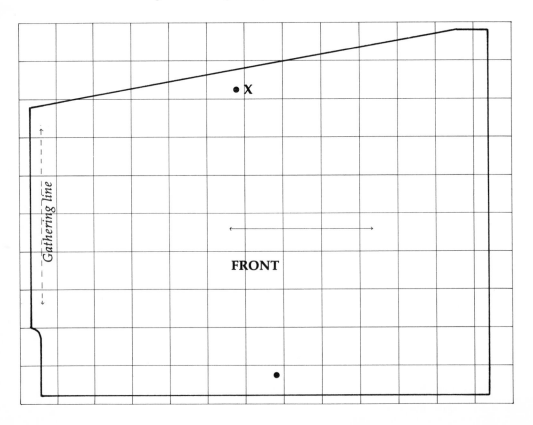

Gathering line

FRONT

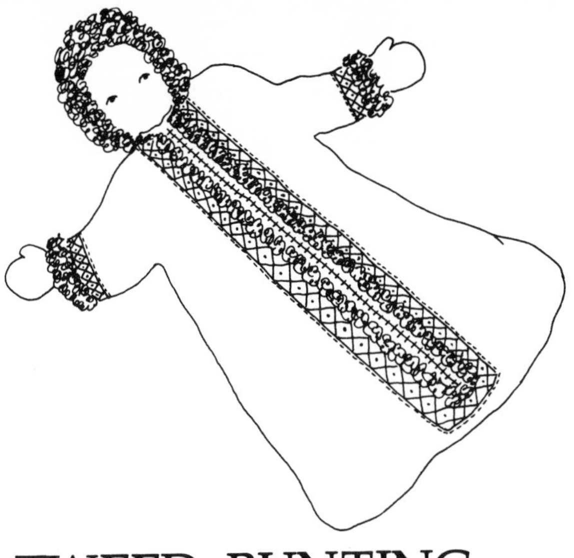

TWEED BUNTING

This bunting is quick to make in multicolored tweed, with braid trim and embroidered looped fringe for a touch of luxury.

SHOWN IN COLOR

SIZE: Birth to 6 months. Bunting measures 15″ across back from underarm to underarm, and 25″ from shoulder to lower edge. Sleeve length is 5″.

MATERIALS: 1½ yds. of 45″-wide multicolor tweed; 4 oz. of 4-ply acrylic knitting worsted to match one of the colors in the tweed (**note:** Acrylic yarn will give the loops a fluffier effect than wool yarn); 2½ yds. of 1″-wide decorative braid; 20″ neckline zipper; 1¾ yds. of 36″-wide lining material (flannel or a calico printed cotton); 1 tapestry needle.

PATTERN: Trace patterns of Embroidered Bunting on page 152 and cut pieces from tweed and lining fabrics, adding ½″ to all edges for seam allowance (2 fronts, 1 back and 1 hood of each fabric).

TO ASSEMBLE: With right sides of tweed fronts together, starting at lower edge, stitch center front seam for 4″, leaving rest of front open for zipper. With right sides of back and front together, stitch lower edge, side and underarm seams. Stitch shoulder and top sleeve seams, leaving 8″ open at center back and 4″ at each center front for neck opening. Turn right side out and press. Fold hood in half crosswise and sew top seam. With right sides together, sew hood to neck edge. Assemble lining in same manner. Sew zipper in tweed bunting.

TO INSERT LINING: See general directions of Royal Blue Bunting on page 109.

LOOPED FRINGE: Use yarn double throughout. Practice loops on a scrap of fabric before working them on bunting.

Step 1: Draw yarn to right side. With left thumb hold yarn down, skip 1/4" of fabric to right and insert needle from right to left, bringing needle up in front of place where yarn emerges from fabric. Using your thumb as a gauge for size of loop, draw yarn through to form a loop over thumb.

Step 2: Remove thumb from loop and hold loop down as shown. Skip 1/4" of fabric to right and insert needle from right to left, bringing needle up in front of last stitch. Draw yarn tight to fasten stitch.

Step 3: Hold yarn down as in Step 1 and make loop as in Step 1. Then make stitch to fasten as in Step 2. Continue in this manner, forming loops at even intervals. Working on bunting, work 3 rows of fringe, close together, around front opening and face edge of hood. Work 3 rows of fringe around sleeves.

Following photograph for placement, sew braid in place around fringe, mitering braid at corners.

LOOPED FRINGE

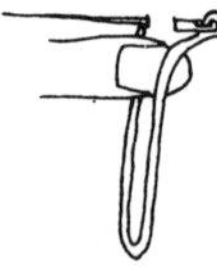

Step 1

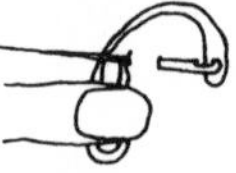

Step 2

Step 3

RED HEART PINCUSHION

This lovely pincushion will keep those pins safely out of reach of little hands. It is worked in tent stitch with a center folk-art motif, inspired by the cross-stitch samplers of yesteryear. The center is left open on the chart to personalize it with your baby's initials. A gingham ruffle finishes it off.

SHOWN IN COLOR

SIZE: Needlepoint area, 5½″ x 6½″.

MATERIALS: Mono needlepoint canvas, 1 piece 9½″ square with 12 spaces per inch; Bucilla needlepoint and crewel wool; 2 (30-yd.) cards white and 5 cards red no. 92; 1 piece red felt for backing 9½″ square; for ruffle: a bias strip of red gingham 4″ x 72″; polyester filling for stuffing; tapestry needle; masking tape.

For Blocking: Soft wooden surface; brown paper (such as a shopping bag); rustproof thumbtacks, or you can use a lightweight staple gun.

GENERAL DIRECTIONS: With a pencil, mark horizontal and vertical center lines on canvas. Tape raw edges of canvas with masking tape to keep them from raveling, or overcast them with thread.

The pincushion is worked in tent or continental stitch (see stitch diagram), which looks like the half cross-stitch.

The Bucilla yarn separates into 3 strands of yarn. Use only 2 strands of yarn throughout.

Follow the chart and color key to work the design. Each little square represents 1 stitch. You can work from the center or in rows. It is easiest to work the white design area first and then to fill in the red background.

STITCH DIAGRAM

Tent or continental stitch

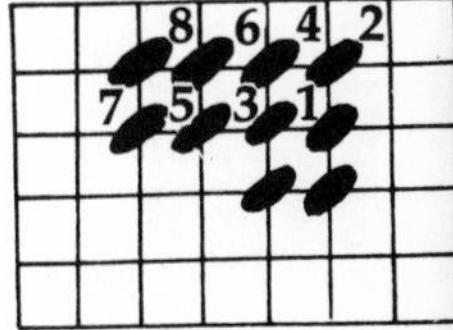

FINISHING:

Blocking: With a pencil and a ruler draw canvas outline on brown paper, making sure the corners are square. Tack paper to wooden surface. Dampen needlepoint and lay canvas right side down on board. Stretch and tack, or staple, work in place along paper outline. Let dry thoroughly.

When dry, unpin and trim to allow for a 1″ seam allowance all around. Cut felt for backing the same size as canvas.

To Make Ruffle: Turn under raw edges ¼″ at short ends of gingham strip. Fold strip lengthwise. Machine-baste through both layers of fabric 1″ from raw edge. Gather by pulling thread until ruffle measures about 22″.

With raw edges together, place ruffle on right side of canvas along edge. Pin and baste ruffle in place just inside needlepoint area, adjusting gathers at lower point and along curves. Stitch ruffle to canvas.

Pin felt to right side of canvas with ruffle in between. Stitch pieces together, making a 1″ seam and leaving a 3″ opening in center of one side for stuffing. Trim seams to ⅜″, clip curves and corners. Turn right side out. Stuff fully. Turn edges of opening in and sew closed.

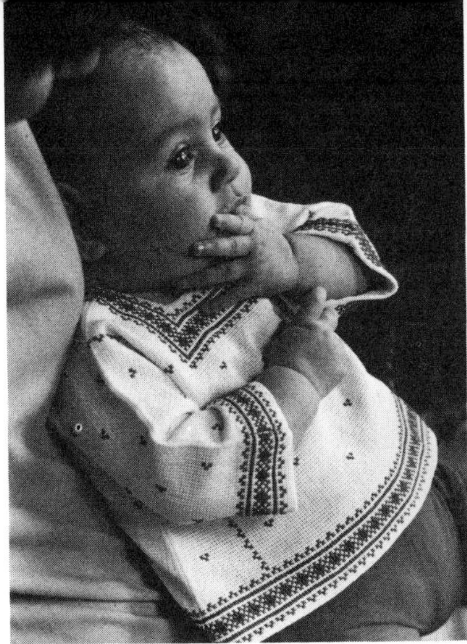

CROSS-STITCH SHIRT

A cool little shirt for boy or girl, decorated with red and blue cross-stitch embroidery on a white background. In the old European tradition, these shirts were originally worn as long nightgowns made of fine homespun linens.

Another version of the same pattern is this short-sleeved top, finished off with buttonhole stitches and embroidered with gaily colored little flowers of your imagination. It would look equally charming in a plain muslin or a bright-colored cotton.

SIZE: 3–6 months. Shirt measures 10″ across at underarms, $8\frac{1}{2}$″ from shoulder to lower edge. Sleeve length is $4\frac{1}{2}$″.
MATERIALS: $\frac{1}{3}$ yd. of 54″-wide Aida even-weave cotton, 22 threads per inch—see page 160 for mail-order resource; 6-strand DMC embroidery floss, 9 skeins red no. 666 and 1 skein blue no. 820; 3 snaps.
CUTTING: Enlarge pattern (see page 22). For front, cut 1 piece on fold; for back, cut 2 pieces; for front facing, cut 1 piece on fold; for back facing, cut 2 pieces. Finish all edges with overhand stitch.
SEWING: Sew shoulder seams of shirt and facing. Press open seams.

Baste off $\frac{1}{2}$″ seam allowance around neck, sleeves and lower edges. Mark center front of shirt.
EMBROIDERY: Follow chart for design and key for colors.

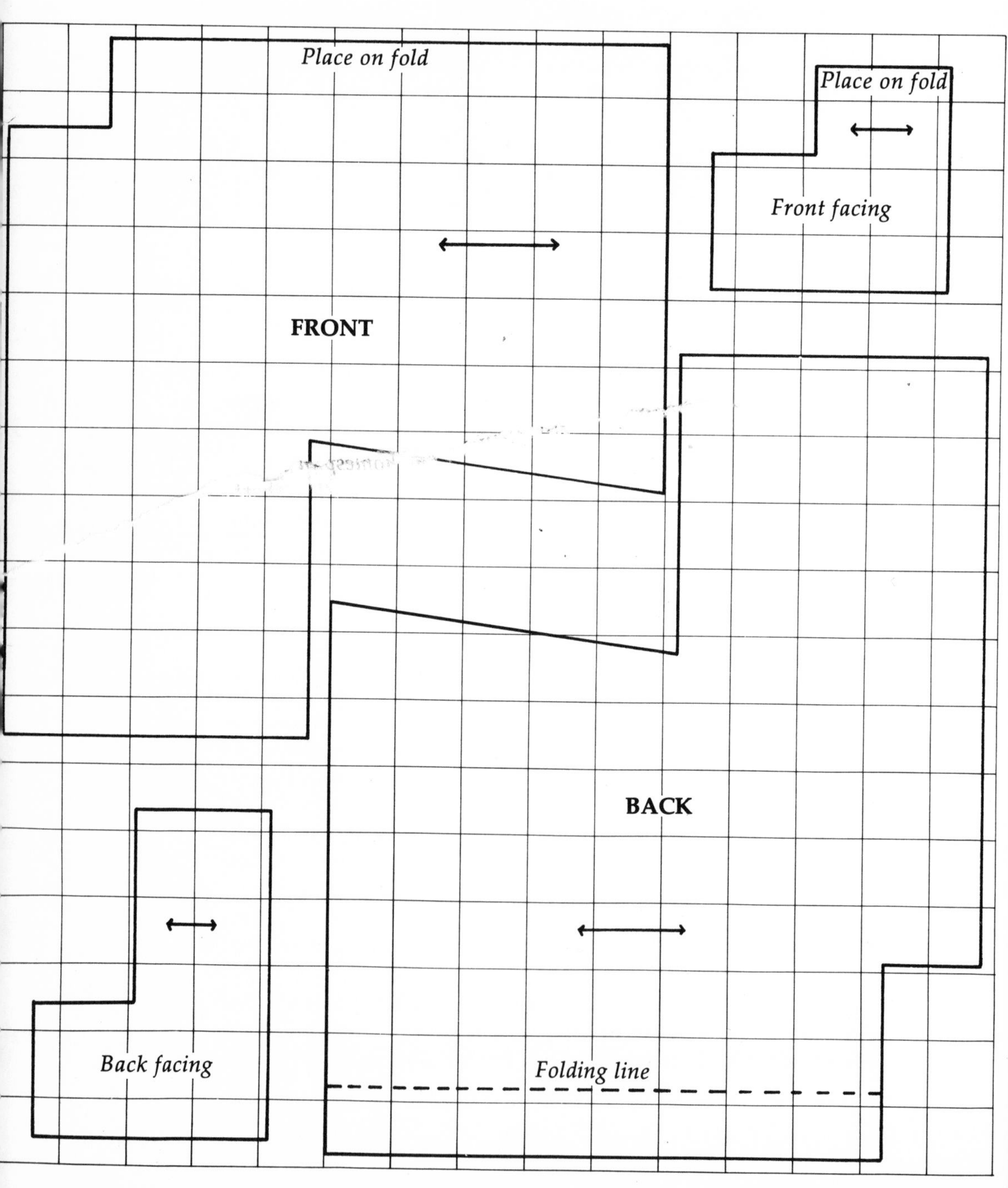
Place on fold
Place on fold
Front facing
FRONT
BACK
Back facing
Folding line

Work each cross-stitch over 2 horizontal and 2 vertical threads, using 3 strands of embroidery floss throughout. See cross-stitch diagram on page 74 on how to execute this stitch. Match center front of shirt and center of design. Starting 24 threads below basting line, work pattern A, repeating the motif between arrows, around neck edge to folding line on back sections, work row B, then pattern C, repeating motif between arrows. Band completed.

Work same band pattern around sleeve edges.

SEWING: With right sides together, sew facing to neck opening. Clip corners, trim seam. Turn facing to wrong side. Tack at corners. Sew underarm and side seams.

EMBROIDERY: Work band pattern as before around lower edge. Work motif E 2¼″ in from neck edge, on both sides of neck opening on front only. Work motif D evenly spaced over front, back and sleeve areas.

SEWING: Fold hems to wrong side on basting line around sleeve and lower edges. Slip-stitch in place. Fold back edges 1″ to inside along fold lines to form facing.

Sew 3 snaps to back edges, first one at back neck opening, the others spaced 2¼″ apart.

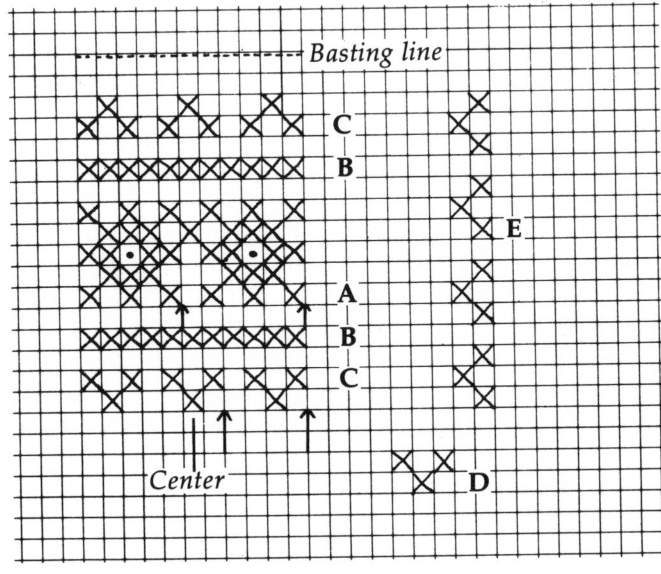

COLOR KEY

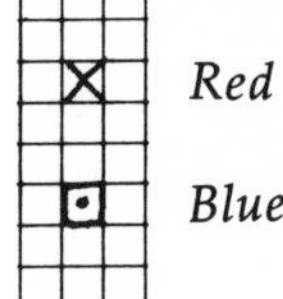

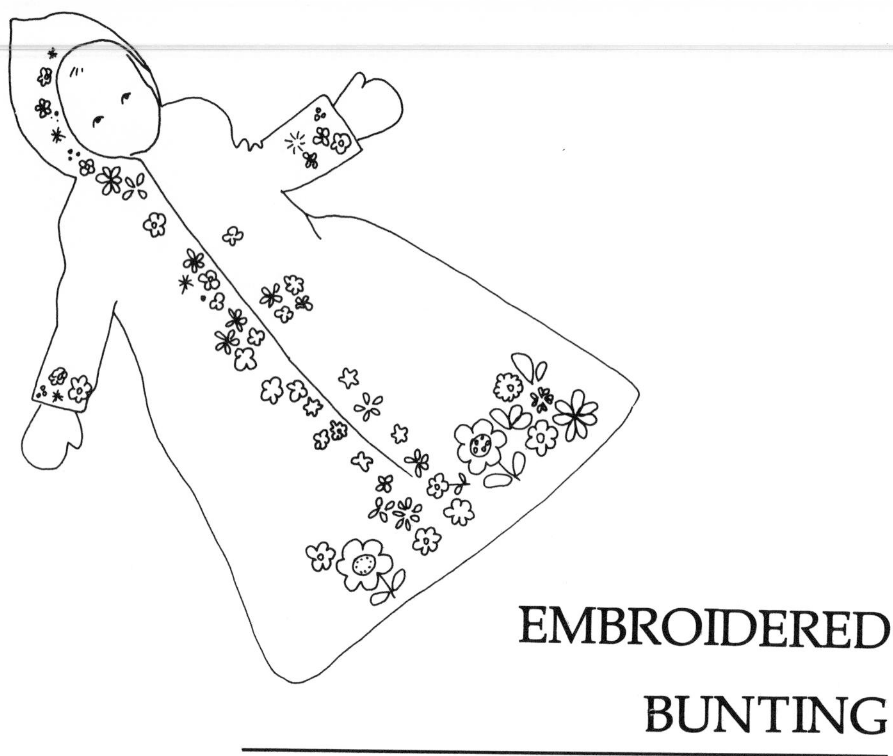

EMBROIDERED BUNTING

This kelly green wool flannel bunting, like a spring meadow, is scattered with multicolored embroidered flowers. Who could resist nature's call to go out with baby and enjoy the first warm days of spring?

SHOWN IN COLOR

SIZE: Birth to 6 months. Bunting measures 15″ across back from underarm to underarm, and 25″ from shoulder to lower edge. Sleeve length is 5″.
MATERIALS: 1½ yds. of 45″-wide kelly green wool flannel; 1¾ yds. of 36″-wide lining material (flannel or printed cotton); 20″ neckline zipper; DMC tapestry yarn: 1 (8¾-yd.) skein each pale blue no. 7313, pink no. 7151, red no. 7107, 2 skeins each purple no. 7708, medium blue no. 7314, green no. 7342, orange no. 7437, yellow no. 7433 and white; dressmaker's carbon paper; tracing paper or clear plastic bag cut open; felt-tipped marker with fine point.
PATTERN: Cut pieces same as for Tweed Bunting on page 145.
EMBROIDERY: With marker, trace embroidered area from

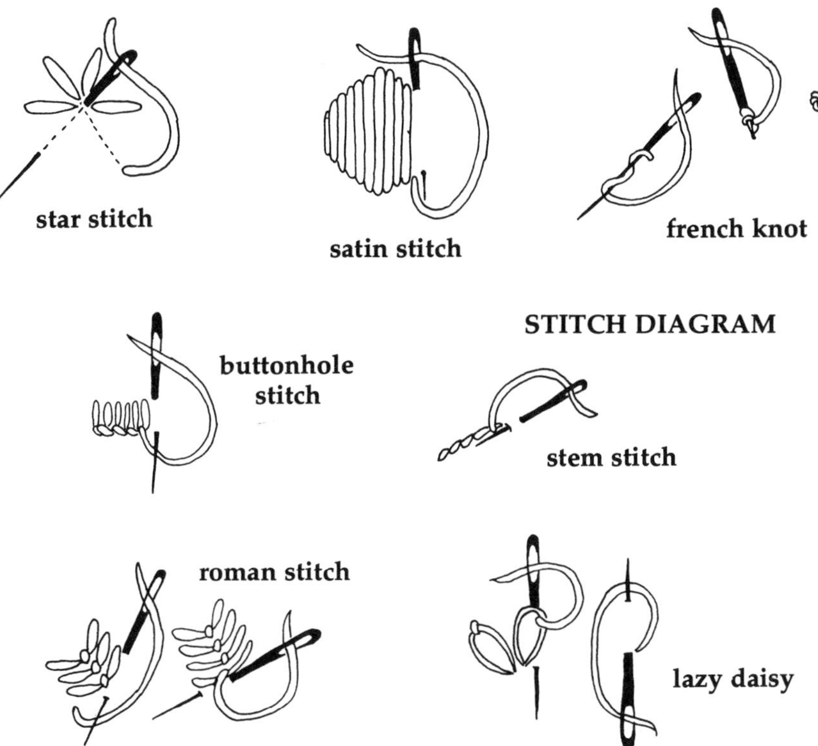

pattern on pages 154–55 onto tracing paper or plastic. Place tracing on bunting, right side up, and carefully slide dressmaker's carbon between bunting and tracing, carbon side down. Pin in place. With semisharp pencil (to avoid excessive tearing of tracing) or point of knitting needle, transfer design to bunting.

Follow keys for colors and stitches and diagrams for working stitches. Where similar motifs are the same color or worked in the same stitch, only 1 motif is marked. **Note:** Half the flowers on the hood are marked, the remaining flowers are worked in the same colors. The flowers are marked with lines indicating the direction in which to work satin stitches. Work embroidery to within ½″ from zipper opening, hood and sleeve edges.

TO ASSEMBLE: See Tweed Bunting on page 145.

TO INSERT LINING: See general directions for Royal Blue Bunting on page 109.

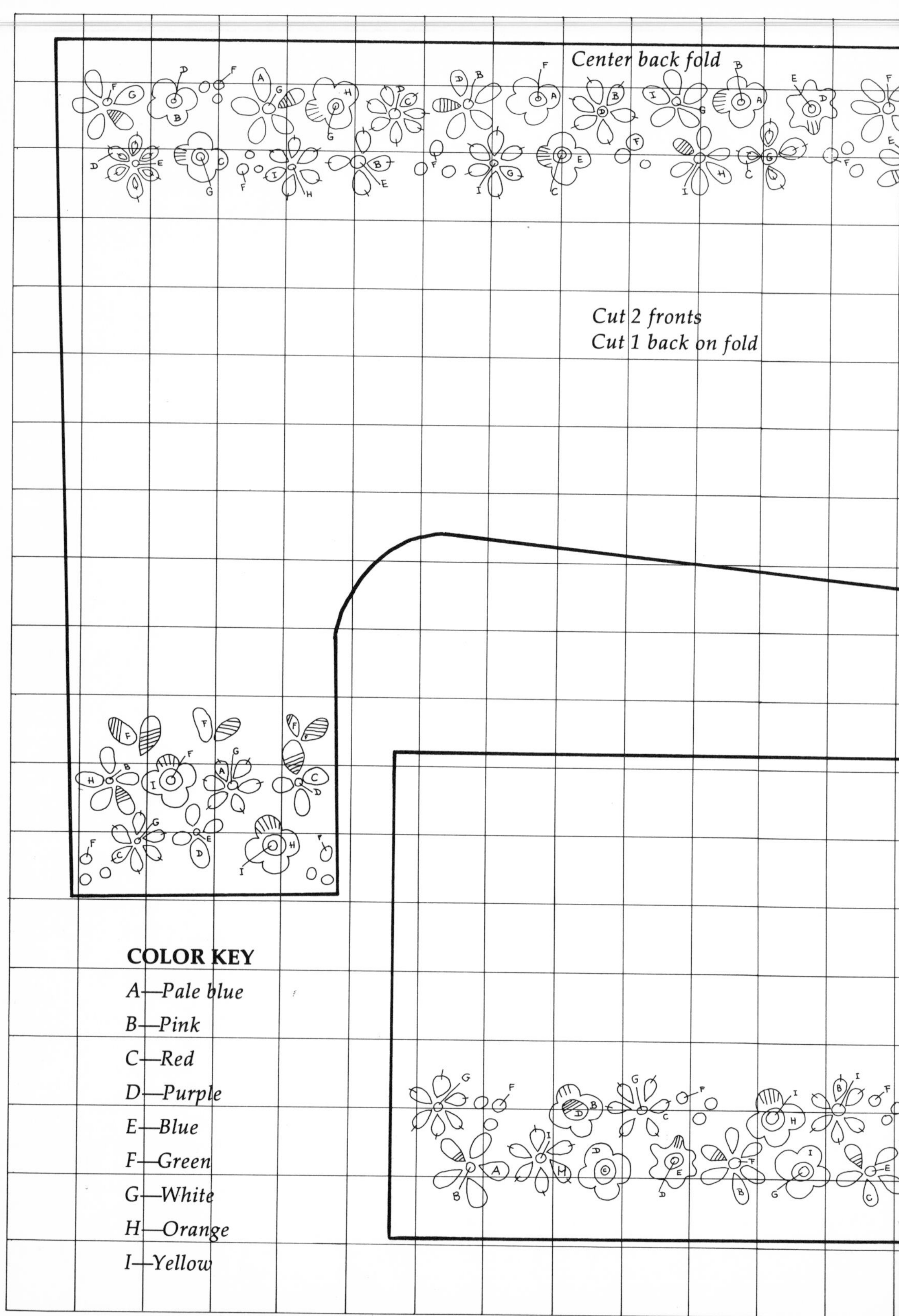
Center back fold
Cut 2 fronts
Cut 1 back on fold
COLOR KEY
A—Pale blue
B—Pink
C—Red
D—Purple
E—Blue
F—Green
G—White
H—Orange
I—Yellow

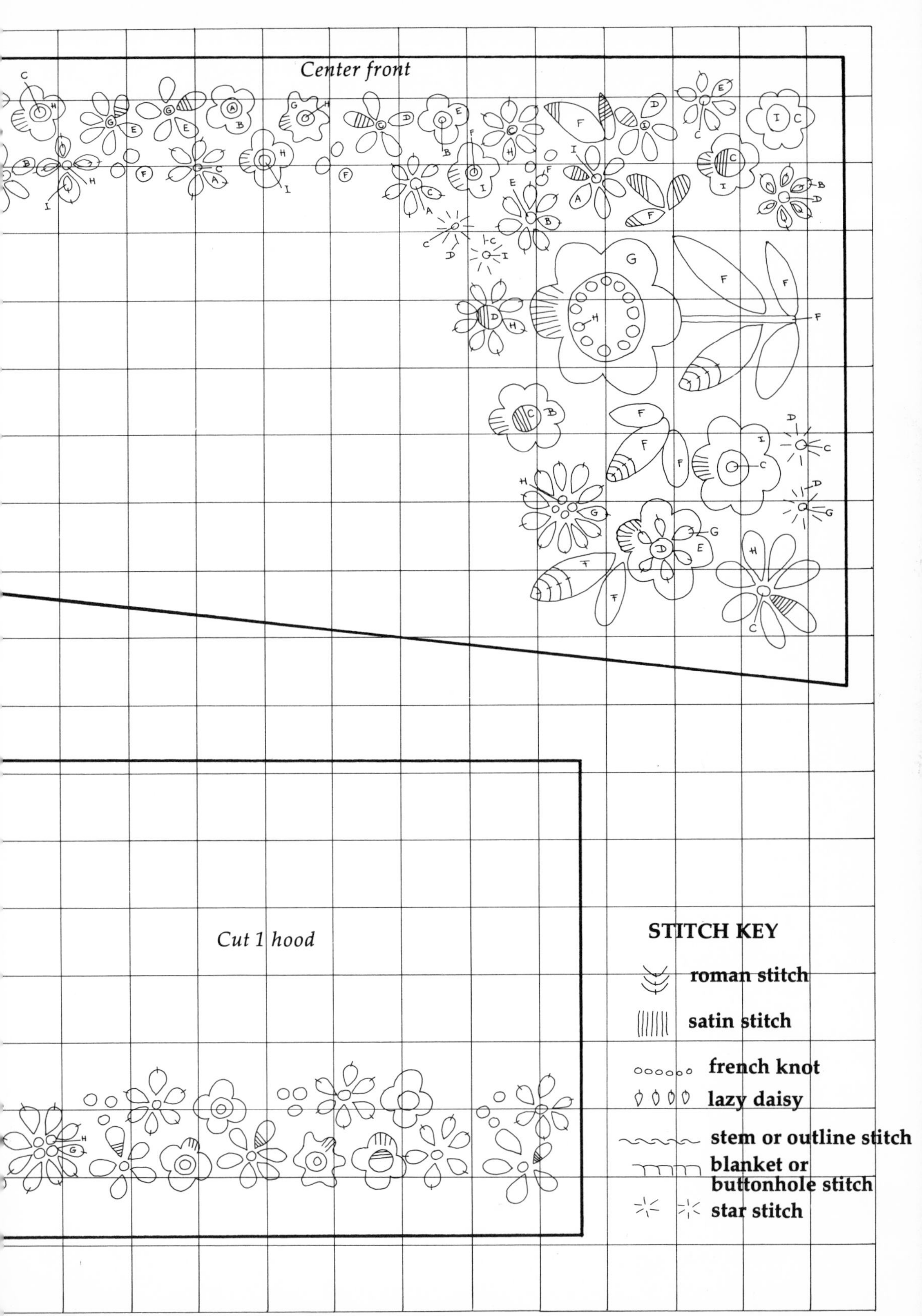

Center front
Cut 1 hood
STITCH KEY
roman stitch
satin stitch
french knot
lazy daisy
stem or outline stitch
blanket or buttonhole stitch
star stitch

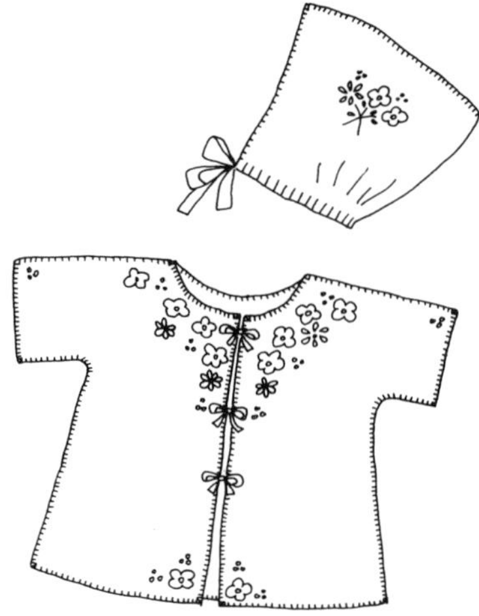

BONNET AND SACQUE

For those of you who can neither knit nor crochet, here is a project to try your hand at. The bonnet and matching sacque, made of cotton flannel, are hemmed and blanket-stitched all around the edges. Then the seams are whipstitched together. Small flowers worked in basic embroidery stitches add a personal touch.

BONNET
SIZE: Infant.
MATERIALS: One blue cotton flannel rectangle, 7½" x 13"; J. and P. Coats de Luxe 6-strand embroidery floss, 2 skeins grass green, 1 skein each lavender and purple; ¾ yd. ¼"-wide lavender satin ribbon; dressmaker's carbon paper; tracing paper or clear plastic bag cut open; felt-tipped marker with fine point.
TO MAKE: Along 2 short edges and 1 long edge of rectangle turn under raw edges ¼", then fold under ¼" once more. Baste.

For casing, turn remaining long edge under ¼"; then fold under ½". Baste.

Using 6 strands of green embroidery floss, work blanket stitch (see page 153) around all edges, being careful to leave ends of casing free.

Fold rectangle crosswise and mark center of each side of bonnet. Enlarge embroidery design (see page 22) and transfer it (see page 124) to center of each side of bonnet with dressmaker's carbon. Following stitch diagram and key for colors, work embroidery with 3 strands of floss.

With lavender, whipstitch over blanket stitch along one short edge, casing and opposite short edge, fold rectangle crosswise with wrong sides together and whipstitch top edges together. Weave ribbon through casing.

SACQUE

Use pattern of Blue Bandanna Kimono (page 135) and shorten to length desired. Work it in the same manner as for bonnet, hemming edges, finishing them in blanket stitch and whipstitching seams together. Embroider, following drawing for position of flowers.

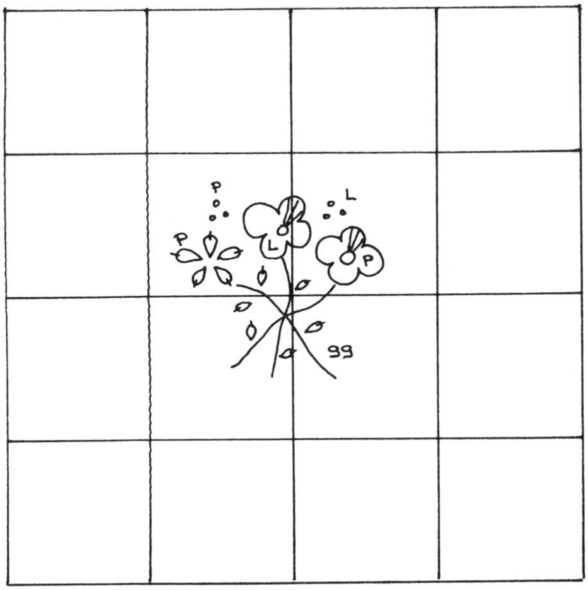

STITCH KEY

ııııı	**satin stitch**
ooo	**french knot**
——	**outline stitch**
⊖	**lazy daisy**

COLOR KEY

L—Lavender

P—Purple

GG—Grass green

SLEEPING BAG

This is a handy item to make and have for use in the carriage or in the car. A snug instant bed.

Make it of fake sheepskin fur and decorate it with exotic ribbons, braid and rickrack.

TO MAKE: Cut 2 rectangles to fit your carriage; round all corners. With furry sides together, sew pieces together, leaving top edges and one third of sides open. Trim.

A LAST-MINUTE PROJECT

A baby can't have too many undershirts. On a hot summer day, it's nice to wear just that. To keep it from looking so underwearish, spruce it up with embroidery—finishing the edges with a blanket-stitch trim, a narrow lace or a crocheted little edging.

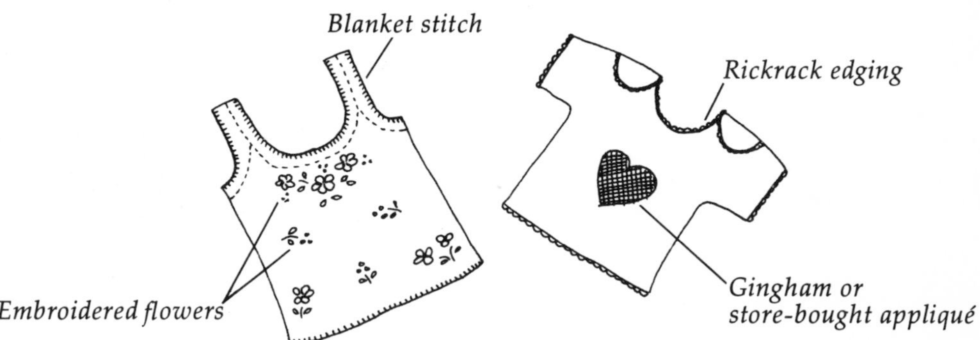

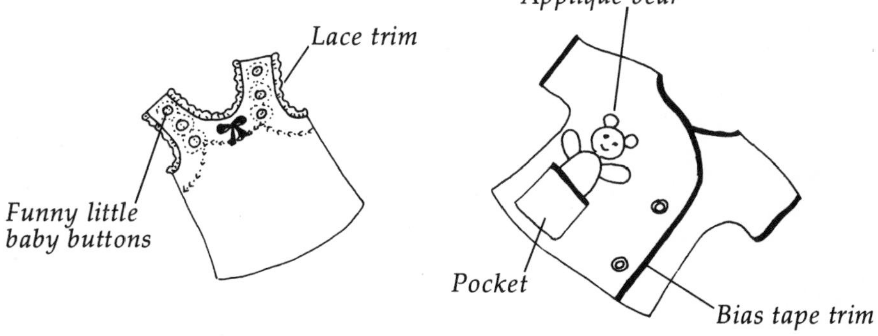

SOURCES

Most of the materials used for the projects in this book are well-distributed and easy to get. The fabrics are your own choice, and notions, needles and hooks are readily available at dime stores.

However, if you still have trouble getting any of the materials mentioned, write to the following addresses for mail order information:

Bear Brand, Bucilla
Merchandise Mailing Service
Box 144
East Meadow, New Jersey 11554

Brunswick
Windy Ways
Brandwood Station
Greenville, South Carolina 29610

Bernat
Art Needlecraft, Inc.
Box 394
Uxbridge, Massachusetts 01569

D.M.C., Aida Evenweave Cotton
Joan Toggitt, Ltd.
246 Fifth Avenue
New York, New York 10001

Write directly to the manufacturers below to find out the location of your nearest dealer:

Coats & Clark's
75 Rockefeller Center
New York, New York 10020

Spinnerin
230 Fifth Avenue
New York, New York 10001